practical
kindness

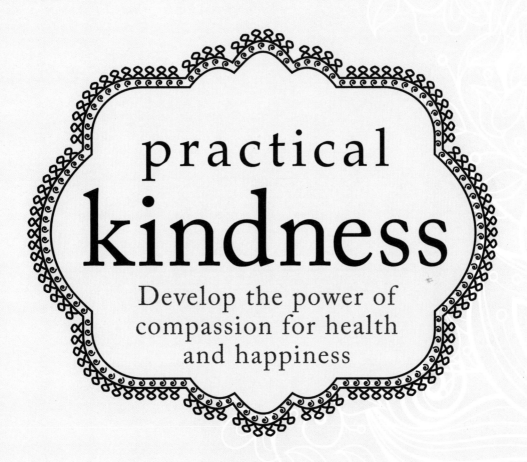

practical
kindness

Develop the power of
compassion for health
and happiness

RAJE S. AIREY

LORENZ BOOKS

contents

INTRODUCTION

There are many reasons why kindness improves your life: better mental health, improved life satisfaction and stronger relationships have all been linked to kindness and generosity, with generous people even living longer.

WHY KINDNESS MATTERS

There is no doubt that human beings can do amazing things. We can probe the furthest reaches of outer space and plumb the depths of the ocean floor. At the touch of a screen we can see, hear and talk to someone on the other side of the world. Distances seem to be getting smaller. People are living longer. Standards of living have improved. Yet despite all our gains we are no happier. By 2020 the World Health Organization predicts that depression will be a significant cause of 'disability' worldwide, second only to heart disease. We have not yet found a way to resolve conflict and warfare, to stop hate crimes or prevent people dying from starvation. And human activity is destroying the planet's ecosystem.

Clearly then we have not yet learnt how to be happy, be at peace and live in harmony – with either ourselves, with one another or with the environment. In his book *The Power of Kindness* (2007) Piero Ferrucci says that 'global cooling' is the problem, referring to the current era as 'the ice age of the heart'. Ferrucci argues that human relationships have become

> *'No-one can live a happy life if he turns everything to his own purpose. Live for others if you want to live for yourself.'*
>
> SENECA

more cool and distant, hurried and impersonal, and that the drive for profit and efficiency is pursued at the expense of human warmth and genuine presence. Many are now saying that the advances in our outer world need to be matched by developments in our inner world. At the Mindfulness Summit in October 2015 for example, Buddhist teacher Jack Kornfield said it is time for modern humanity to develop emotional intelligence, and to cultivate kindness, wisdom and care.

This means we have a choice: do we continue along the same old tracks or are we prepared to push out the boundaries and commit to an intention (even if we do not always succeed) to behave with generosity, kindness and compassion?

WHAT IS KINDNESS?

Kindness is an active expression of care, concern, warmth and generosity that asks for nothing in return. If we do something to get something back, it is not kindness but a deal, a transaction, a manipulation. Connected with its sister qualities such as compassion, empathy and sympathy, kindness is allowing the wisdom of the heart, giving it space to breathe, to feel and to connect with ourselves, with others and with the environment.

When elevated to the level of compassion, kindness becomes about wanting to reduce suffering, helping others who are in pain or who are less fortunate than ourselves. All too often we are in too much of a hurry to really pay attention to other people, too busy listening to self-criticism and dealing with our negative thoughts and feelings. We have lost touch with ourselves and by definition we are out of touch with others. By focusing on kindness and compassion we can gradually turn the tables. We can start changing our outlook, focusing on cooperation rather than competition, on connection rather than isolation, on taking a broader perspective rather than remaining within the narrow confines of our own lives. Such an agenda is based in compassionate-mindfulness, which many believe can stimulate change from the inside out. This does not promise a dramatic quick fix, but if we commit to practise kindness in our lives, it can help us reach a new level of consciousness, to become kinder, happier and at peace with ourselves and the world.

Dispelling assumptions

There are many mistaken views about kindness and compassion. Many think they don't deserve it. That it's 'ok for others, but not for me'. Or that kindness is not 'sexy' or cool. In post-industrial consumer society where profit rules, compassion is not seen as a virtue to be cultivated but as something to be reined in and controlled. Men may fear that being too kind denotes lack of masculinity, to risk being thought a bit of a wimp. Or else it can be written off as a hippy dippy 'group hug' sort of thing. For many, kindness has been seen as a feminine trait and either elevated to saintly status by public figures such as Princess Diana or Mother Teresa or hidden in the home and nursery, something we take for granted and deemed not very interesting or worth talking about.

None of these attitudes are right. Far from being a soft and fluffy option, there is a hard edge to kindness and compassion that depending on how far we choose to take it will inevitably challenge our self-beliefs and the way we relate to ourselves, to others, and to our environment. Being kind and compassionate does not mean that anything goes. Instead it asks us to take responsibility for our choices and actions and encourages the development of moral qualities such as courage and wisdom. These qualities involve hard work, a commitment to developing as people, learning how to become more tolerant, generous and empathic, and to open our hearts.

Having a kind and compassionate orientation also means developing our capacity for non-judgemental acceptance, for gratitude and forgiveness – first and foremost towards ourselves, for often we are our own harshest critics. It also means being willing to raise our game above simple survival instincts to a level where we value connection, and working for the good of all and not just for ourselves.

THE TREE OF KINDNESS

This book is divided into three sections, each forming part of a 'tree of kindness' that can grow from small beginnings and shelter us from the storms of life. The first section (roots) deals with the foundations of kindness. It begins by setting the scene, providing an overview of social, historical and religious aspects to kindness before looking at contemporary understandings based on perspectives from neuroscience and psychology.

Section two (branches) outlines five key 'pathways to kindness' that show how kindness operates at a personal level. This covers self-compassion, how we can become more kind towards our bodies and in the mind, when dealing with difficult emotions and in nurturing the soul.

The final section (fruits and seeds), explores the ripple effects of kindness, extending out from beyond ourselves to our relationships with others and the society we live in, before looking at our relationship to nature and how we can express kindness to the earth.

Kindness breeds kindness: through being on the receiving end of kindness we are more likely to be kind. The happiness people derive from giving to others creates positive feedback, positive feelings inspire further generosity, which in turn fuels greater happiness. Aside from being too wrapped up in our concerns to notice other people's needs, we may just be out of practice. Kindness is like a muscle that needs to be strengthened through repeated use.

Throughout the book there are plenty of practical ideas, compassion-based mindfulness exercises, and suggestions for bringing more kindness into your everyday life. It is hoped that the book will become an indispensable and easily accessible resource and that through dipping into it regularly you will gain a greater understanding of what kindness is, how it works, and why it is important. I hope you will become inspired to try out the ideas to help you become more kind and compassionate – towards yourself, towards others and towards the earth. By making small changes and through acts of kindness we can all help build a happier and more peaceful society for the next generation.

ROOTS
THE FOUNDATIONS
OF KINDNESS

Kind hearts are the gardens,
Kind thoughts are the roots,
Kind words are the flowers,
Kind deeds are the fruits.
Take care of your garden
And keep out the weeds,
Fill it with sunshine,
Kind words and kind deeds.

HENRY WADSWORTH LONGFELLOW

BEING HAPPY,
living kindly

DIFFERENT PERSPECTIVES

As societies become more prosperous the perennial question is asked of how best to live a good life and be happy. It seems clear however that increased wealth and security doesn't necessarily mean contentment.

Because we are social beings who are shaped by experience, our answers to this question will inevitably be influenced by the culture and age in which we live. Writing in *The Selfish Society* (2010), psychotherapist Sue Gerhardt argues that it is the social and historical context that shapes our values and determines what we regard as normal behaviour, making a distinction between societies that are based on individualist or collective values.

In today's era of advanced capitalism, modern society is largely based on competitive values, which can be expressed as a me-and-mine-first mentality. This can give rise to a type of self-centred narcissism, with over-consumption, a lack of social cohesion and little sense of collective responsibility, perhaps leading to what some see as the unacceptable side of capitalism and the crises in banking and in political corruption.

As a reaction to this many people are campaigning to raise the profile of heart-centred values such as kindness, compassion and generosity, love and friendship, social justice and care for others. A 'Kindness Revolution' is quietly taking place, demonstrated by organizations such as 'Just Giving', a global online social platform set up to promote and support charitable giving and fundraising, as well as the World Kindness Movement (WKM). We do not become happier by having more money or spending it on more 'stuff'. In fact research suggests exactly the opposite: that as our incomes have risen, we have actually become unhappier. Research shows that one of the best ways of increasing our own happiness is to do things that make other people happy – that it pays to be kind.

World Kindness Day

The 13th November has been designated World Kindness Day by the World Kindness Movement. The purpose of the day is to focus on the common threads that bind humanity.

WORLD KINDNESS MOVEMENT

The WKM is an international movement with no political or religious affiliations. The movement started in Japan in 2007 with a mission to inspire people towards greater care and kindness and to help nations connect to create a kinder, more just world. The WKM encourages people to establish kindness movements in their own countries and to collaborate on global initiatives with the aim of eventually uniting all the world's nations under a 'Coalition of the Good-willing'. The international Random Acts of Kindness (RAK) Foundation is connected with the WKM and is dedicated to creating a culture of kindness in schools, homes and communities with random acts of kindness.

A HISTORY OF KINDNESS

Understanding the importance of kindness and that relationships have an important role to play in achieving happiness is not new. In the classical world, the Epicureans and the Stoics were two dominant and rival schools of philosophy, both with strongly held beliefs on the nature and purpose of friendship.

Epicurus (341–270 BCE) believed friendship was the foundation for a satisfying life: '*Of all the things which wisdom has contrived which contribute to a blessed life, none is more important, more fruitful, than friendship.*' (Cicero, quoting Epicurus). Epicureans emphasised that life is about personal relationships and that friendship is an important ingredient for happiness. Friends were not regarded as an optional extra but as absolutely necessary, helping us in times of trouble and providing companionship.

The Stoics however took the value of friendship to another level. Stoic philosophers such as Seneca and Hierocles believed that the bonds of friendship were integral to developing as a human being, seeing friendship in more altruistic than pragmatic terms. Although the Stoics acknowledged Aristotle's belief that love begins first with the self, they interpreted this in non-individualistic terms, developing a concept of 'self-and-others' known as *oikeiosis*. Derived from *oikos* meaning 'home', the term has no direct translation but regards the individual as the centre point of concentric circles, the innermost circles comprising close relatives, followed by friends and neighbours, broadening out to encompass a larger circle of the whole of humanity, and ultimately the largest outer circle of all sentient beings. The aim is to reduce distinction between the circles.

Oikeiosis formed the basis of a moral philosophy in which attachment to others was not only deemed necessary for companionship but more importantly in order for people to fulfil their humanity. Emperor Marcus Aurelius (121–180 AD), himself a Stoic, believed that citizens were united by reason and mutual affection.

SYMPATHY BREAKTHROUGHS

Historian Jonathan Glover suggests that history can be thought of as a contest between cruelty and compassion, with examples of kindness taking over. George Orwell's famous refusal to shoot a fascist enemy in the Spanish civil war was after a face-to-face encounter in which a half-dressed soldier came running past holding up his trousers: '*I did not shoot partly because of that detail about the trousers. I had come here to shoot at 'Fascists'; but a man who is holding up his trousers isn't a 'Fascist', he is visibly a fellow creature, similar to yourself, and you don't feel like shooting at him.*' Many other examples have been recorded of soldiers disobeying orders when confronted by the humanity or vulnerability of the enemy.

The evolution of kindness

Charles Darwin (1809–82) believed that emotional qualities such as sympathy, caring for others, belonging in groups, and reciprocal acts of kindness and generosity, are our strongest instincts. He also claimed that our evolved tendencies towards goodness are stronger than those of self-preservation because they are themselves linked with survival. This led to Darwin's assertion that social or maternal instincts are stronger than any other instinct or motive. There is some evidence to support this, possibly because parents need to be kind and compassionate to raise their children well.

RELIGIOUS TRADITIONS

Finding ways to deal with suffering and achieve happiness is addressed in different ways by many religions. The problem of human suffering is perhaps most clearly explicated in Buddhism, where it is regarded as the 'first noble truth'. Kindness and compassion are central to Buddhist teaching, offering a way to relieve personal pain and promote peaceful cooperation with one another.

Encouraging a sense of collective responsibility and being compassionate towards others is a core teaching not only in Buddhism but in all the world's religions as well as in the wisdom traditions of indigenous people, where societies tend to be run on collectivist principles.

In ancient China for example, Confucius (551–479 BCE) taught that we should not do to others what we would not like to have done to ourselves, while Taoist philosopher Lao Tzu (d.531 BC) said that *'kindness in giving creates love'*. Hinduism has a pantheon of deities, with loving

> *'Kindness in words creates confidence. Kindness in thinking creates profoundness. Kindness in giving creates love.'*
>
> LAO TZU

kindness being one of the most prominent qualities of the gods found in the Rig Veda, the holy Hindu scriptures. It is through their kindness that the gods bestow blessings and offer protection. For example Tara is the goddess of infinite kindness while Shiva is the lord of mercy and kindness. Hinduism is a compassionate religion and treats all living beings, humans, animals and insects, as aspects of divine creation.

In Judaism the rabbis of the Talmud (Yevamot 79a) consider kindness to be one of the three distinguishing characteristics of a Jew, and a favourite Talmudic name of God is *Rachmana*, meaning 'Compassionate One'. The most consistent and all-embracing act of the Jewish faith is referred to as *chesed* (which means kindness), with the overarching goal being to develop this trait, most clearly manifested by giving.

In the Christian tradition, St Paul lists kindness as one of the nine traits considered to be the fruits of the Spirit (Galatians 5:22), while in the Parable of the Good Samaritan Jesus exhorts his followers to '*love thy neighbour as thyself*' (Mark 12:31), showing how an act of kindness has the power to cross ethnic barriers and turn enemies into friends.

Islam places great store on neighbourly values, with Muhammed saying '*No one is a believer unless his neighbour feels safe from harm on his account.*' Muslims are encouraged to treat their neighbours in a way that reflects the spirit of Islam and to show tolerance towards other faiths.

The religions of indigenous peoples are based on a belief in the sacredness of nature and the interconnectedness of all things. Traditional eco-spirituality is as old as humanity itself, with qualities such as kindness, compassion and generosity extended beyond human beings looking out for one another to include all life forms, a reverence for the sacredness of Life.

Ubuntu

There is a story that an anthropologist proposed a game to children of an African tribe. Putting a basket of fruit under a tree he told the children that the first one to reach the basket would win all the fruit. The children joined hands, all ran together and collected the fruit as a group. The anthropologist asked the children why they hadn't tried to be the first to the fruit. The children replied: 'Ubuntu, how can one of us be happy if all the others are sad?' Ubuntu is an ancient African tribal word meaning human-ness; human kindness; humanity toward others. It is a philosophy that says 'I am what I am because of who we all are.' Ubuntu is interconnectedness.

WIRED
to be kind

THE SCIENCE OF EMOTIONS

The question of how best to live a good life and be happy is a universal human concern. To decide whether we are mostly compassionate social beings or selfish ones we need to understand how our brains work.

In his book *The Selfish Gene* (1976) Richard Dawkins contradicts Darwin's claim that human beings are fundamentally pro-social saying, 'Let us try to teach generosity and altruism, because we are born selfish'. Through studying the brain and the body's chemical systems, however, we now know that human beings are not only primed for self-preservation but are also wired to be kind. In a sense Dawkins and Darwin may both be right.

TRICKY BRAIN
Paul Gilbert is a Fellow of the British Psychological Society and a foremost researcher into the social contexts for compassion, having set up the 'Compassionate Mind Foundation' to promote research in this area. He believes that learning how to manage our brain is the biggest and most difficult challenge facing humanity. To grasp that argument we need a basic understanding of the brain's structure and evolutionary history.

The human brain is complex, built over many millions of years in order to meet the challenges of changing environments. Based on the work of Dr Paul Maclean, an American neuroscientist, the so-called 'triune brain' has three areas: the reptilian (seat of instincts), mammalian (seat of emotions) and human (seat of reasoning). These areas layer on top of each other, evolving at different periods of our history.

Paul Gilbert argues that our evolved brain is tricky because of its basic design, making it liable to be easily triggered into destructive behaviours. At the bottom we are wired to survive, with a defining characteristic of the mammalian brain being to form groups (herds) and hierarchies. This leads to a built-in bias

> *'Evolution has made our brains highly sensitive to external and internal kindness. Specific brain areas are focused on directing and responding to kindness and compassion.'*
>
> PAUL GILBERT

within the brain for kin preferences (nepotism) as well as within-group preferences (tribalism). We can see evidence of mammalian brain bias for example in rivalries between gangs or sports teams, or when religious faiths differentiate between believers and non-believers. Generally we find it easier to be kind and to care for those within our group (whether social, political, national or religious), but it takes more effort to extend kindness to those outside it.

Unless we can access the emotional intelligence of the newer human brain, we are subject to being hijacked by our older, faster brain impulses. Our first, quickest response is instinctive and emotional.

We have to purposefully bring the slower-thinking human brain layer online if we want to gain self-mastery. Reason alone won't do it, instead if we can mindfully access the part of the brain built for kindness, also known as the 'soothing system', we can access our emotional intelligence.

Beyond our circle

The decision to be kind and humane, particularly to those who are outside our immediate circle of trust, means tapping into the 'higher' human brain which is where empathy and higher-order social skills are located.

REGULATING EMOTIONS

Emotions, rather than reasons, are what guide our motives and give our life meaning. Emotional regulation theory identifies three types of emotional sub-systems, while neuroplasticity suggests brain patterns can be rewired.

EMOTIONAL REGULATION THEORY
The three emotional sub-systems are the threat system, the drive system, and the soothing system. Each system is associated with different brain regions and distinct feelings, motivations, purposes and neurochemistry. Paul Gilbert has pioneered a 'three circle model' based on these systems that form the basis of Compassion Focused Therapy. The model explains how human beings manage or regulate their emotions, switching between different states. The model argues that people can be in states of 'threat' (focused on danger), 'drive' (with a mindset attuned towards achievement or competition), or 'soothing' (which promotes safeness and feelings of interpersonal connectedness).

The threat system is associated with the amygdala set of neurons and fight-flight-freeze-appease, a rapid better-safe-than-sorry response. Here our primary concern

is survival (act first, think about it later). Many things can trigger the threat system, from the way someone speaks to us (kindly or harshly), to anxieties around work. We can mitigate the threat system by going into drive or soothing mode.

The drive system is connected with the brain's limbic system and is about goals, motivation and reward. If we have anxieties around work for example, we might start putting in longer hours in order to turn the threat system down or off.

The soothing system is associated with the higher brain and is about contentment, feeling safe and connected. Compassion and kindness are part of this system. So instead of working longer hours we could exercise self-compassion with a loving-kindness mindfulness practice or feel soothed through the kindness and reassurance of people we trust.

THE POWER OF THOUGHT

Sometimes referred to as 'molecules of emotion', neuropeptides are chemicals produced in the brain in response to our thoughts and feelings. As these chemicals circulate around the bloodstream they carry information to different parts of the body, impacting us at a cellular and genetic level. Studies show for example that after an injury, stress can cause some genes that are needed to help the body repair itself to 'switch off' or decrease their activity, making wounds slower to heal. The opposite of stress is calm. So it is no surprise that meditation techniques or relaxing practices such as yoga or t'ai chi or anything that involves slow, regular mindful breathing actually helps to deactivate the genes that produce 'stress' hormones. This means our thoughts, attitudes, beliefs and emotions have a direct effect on our physiology, making it impossible to separate the mind from the body. Kind thoughts also stimulate their own neuropeptides, one of which is oxytocin, the feel-good hormone.

Neuroplasticity

Because of something known as 'neuroplasticity' we know that the brain is malleable, that we can literally 'change our minds', altering the chemical structure and neural pathways of the brain on the basis of our thoughts, feelings, intentions, and behaviours. This capacity to change the structure of our brain goes on right until the very end of life, meaning it is never too late to create new habits or modify old ones. So while the brain is already wired for compassion, we can take steps to purposefully strengthen and improve that wiring through things such as acts of kindness.

THE HEALING POWER

Kindness potentially makes us happier and healthier. Compassionate mind states are calming and are characterised by a slowing down of the heart rate – the opposite of which occurs during times of stress.

It is thought that experiencing kindness may release endorphins, the body's natural painkillers. We also have mirror neurons, that register what others are thinking and feeling and reflect what they see. Sometimes referred to as the building blocks of empathy, mirror neurons give us the capacity to feel with another on an emotional, subjective level, prompting us to relieve the suffering of others in part to make ourselves feel better.

Empathy is thought to be the precursor to compassion, a state where we not only feel with the other but where we know that we want the other person's suffering to end and are motivated to do something to help. Feeling better when we help someone also affects our brain chemistry, producing elevated levels of dopamine in the brain, giving what is sometimes referred to as a 'Helper's High'.

KINDNESS AND OXYTOCIN

Also known as the molecule of kindness or love hormone, oxytocin has many benefits. Research shows that it makes people more generous, seem more attractive and makes us more trusting. It also has physical benefits such as improving digestion, speeding up healing and lowering blood pressure. Animals, particularly dogs, help us produce oxytocin. When we play with a dog the oxytocin levels increase, showing the reciprocal benefit of behaving with loving kindness. Oxytocin also has the power to reduce free radicals and inflammation.

THE NERVE OF KINDNESS

There is some evidence of a strong link between compassion and the activity of the vagus nerve, referred to by Steve Porges, a physiological psychologist, as the body's 'caretaking' organ, calling it the nerve of compassion or kindness. The vagus nerve is part of the 'slow down and relax' parasympathetic nervous system (PNS) and is responsible for regulating all the body's major organs and key body systems.

Originating at the top of the spinal column the vagus nerve is actually a collection of nerves, residing in the chest and winding its way through the body; the word 'vagus' meaning 'wandering' in Latin. The nerve helps to stimulate the compassion system,

to slow down our heart rate and connect with oxytocin receptors. It also controls inflammation levels in the body. This in turn may be why kindness is thought to slow down the ageing process.

The vagus nerve is not only connected with physiological processes but is also intimately connected with how we relate to one another. When we feel emotionally moved, and experience a feeling of warmth in the chest or a lump in the throat, or when we give a soothing sigh, it is the vagus nerve that is at work.

The vagus nerve links directly to the nerves that tune our ears to human speech, coordinate eye contact and regulate emotional expressions. Studies have shown that higher 'vagal tone' is associated with greater closeness with others and more altruistic behaviour. It has also been shown that those with a high vagal tone are better able to cope with the stresses and strains of modern life, helping people manage bereavement for example. People suffering from severe depression on the other hand show low vagal tone. If depressed we are much more likely to be inwardly focused and preoccupied with our personal pain, making it more difficult to show compassion for others.

'Whether you're being kind or showing compassion, you are changing your brain... this is one of the most exciting neuroscience discoveries of the 21st century.'

DAVID HAMILTON

HOW WE
become kind

LEARNING TO LOVE

The ways that significant people respond to us as children create patterns of response that become hardwired into the brain. The experiences we have in early life inform the way we feel about ourselves later.

We know that our children will become the adults of tomorrow, but what influences how they will turn out? Why do some people seem more able to feel empathy and show kindness than others? What motivates people to behave in either selfish or pro-social ways? And to what extent are people products of their environment or their genetic inheritance? Perspectives from psychology and neuroscience can shed light on these questions, giving us an understanding of the complex interplay between our genetic makeup, learned behaviour and the impact of early life experiences. It also indicates what is needed for healthy human development and how seeds for qualities like kindness are sown early on.

OUR FIRST RELATIONSHIPS

How we treat ourselves (and others) depends, in part, on how we were raised, an idea that is central in traditional

'In order to develop normally after birth, we need parents who will tend to our needs, help us learn to manage our emotions ... and make us feel safe in the world.'

JOSEPH BURCO

psychoanalytic thinking. In particular the 'object relations' school shifted attention from Freud's focus on the oedipal phase (c3–7 years) to the very early, pre-verbal period. The British psychoanalyst and paediatrician Donald Winnicott (1896–1971) emphasised the importance of kind and nurturing first relationships: *'The foundations of health are laid down by the ordinary mother in her ordinary loving care of her own baby.'* Winnicott coined the phrase, 'the good enough mother', a concept that today would include parents of either gender as well as grandparents or any significant carer.

We don't need perfect parents, only ones that are 'good enough'. But when things go wrong children are unable to develop as they normally would. And as psychoanalyst Joseph Burco says, we know this on an intuitive, deeply felt fundamental level.

GOOD ENOUGH PARENTING
Biologically we are wired to connect and establish emotional bonds, or attachments with others. Evidence of attachment-seeking behaviours are evident straight from birth when babies coo, gurgle, or smile for instance. Such 'cute' behaviour is designed to evoke an emotionally warm response so that the baby gets looked after. Crying and signs of distress are intended to elicit a kind and caring response – signs that the baby needs care and attention.

When parents (and others) show an interest in and have fun with their children, and can validate and explore their child's feelings (including the 'negative' ones) without becoming critical or making the child feel 'wrong', children learn that they are loved and valued for who they are. Through experiencing emotional and physical affection, warmth, kindness and understanding, children learn to feel intrinsically safe. This means they can readily access the soothing compassion system when facing difficulties later on in life and find it relatively easy to have empathy for themselves and others.

It is difficult being a parent. There is no definitive rulebook and people tend to draw on what they learned growing up unless they make a determined effort to try something else. When things go wrong it is important to stress that this is not necessarily anyone's fault. Generally speaking parents strive to do their best for their children but when they themselves lack the necessary support and are struggling with their own lives it comes as no surprise that they will inevitably make mistakes. The important thing is not to become self-critical, but to learn how to become more tolerant, patient and kind with ourselves and with our children.

The good news is that whatever type of parenting we experienced, as adults we can develop a learned secure attachment pattern. One way to do this is to construct a coherent narrative about the past and face up to the emotional pain we have experienced rather than hoping it will all go away. This can be done in the context of a kind and caring relationship either with a professional or with a partner. Learning self-compassion and practising mindfulness can also help us learn to become more self-accepting, self-aware and more secure in ourselves.

> '*We now know that even genes can be turned on and off in a baby's brain, depending on the amount of and type of affection the child receives early in life.*'
>
> GILBERT AND CHODEN

EMOTIONAL INTELLIGENCE

The last decades have increasingly recognised the importance of human connection and the role of emotions in promoting psychological health and wellbeing. In his book *Emotional Intelligence* (1995), Daniel Goleman argues that traditional methods of measuring intelligence (IQ) are too narrow and not necessarily predictors of happiness and success, but that emotional intelligence requires the effective awareness and management of one's own emotions as well as those of others. Emotional intelligence teaches us that qualities such as kindness and compassion are fundamental life-forces that enable us to appreciate and develop connections.

PARENTING THE BRAIN

Neuroscience show us that the emotional environment plays a very significant role in the way a child's brain develops, in particular influencing the way neural connections are formed. The basic 'scaffolding' of the brain's neural pathways is built in the womb, based on the genetic blueprint inherited from the parents, but how the gene store is activated is very experience dependent. This is because much of the infant brain develops after birth and is very open to being sculpted by positive or negative parent interactions.

In particular there are very few neural connections in the 'higher' brain, particularly the orbitofrontal cortex which grows mostly after birth and begins to mature around the age of one. This area of the brain is connected with social and emotional intelligence and how we are parented greatly influences how this area of the brain develops. Brain scans of some institutionalised orphaned babies for example, who received basic physical care but were deprived of attention, affection and nurturing, showed undeveloped 'black holes' in the temporal lobes region, the part of the brain responsible for processing and regulating emotions. In contrast the brain scans of children who have received loving parenting show correspondingly few black areas, meaning that the temporal lobes are active, predicting better social intelligence.

Passing on the love

Children who are brought up in a consistently caring, kind and loving way are most likely to develop into nurturing, compassionate and unselfish people who can experience empathy for someone else. This will be evident in their play very early on.

WISDOM AND
compassion

MINDFUL KINDNESS

With its roots in Buddhist insight meditation, mindfulness has been practised in the East for thousands of years, and is based on the principle of focusing awareness on the present moment.

In Western society mindfulness has become a bit of a buzzword, an approach that can help us cope better with the stresses and strains of modern life. While there are many definitions of mindfulness, it can be understood as becoming curious and paying attention to our moment-to-moment experience, to the thoughts, feelings and bodily sensations that arise within us without judging what's happening or trying to change anything.

It is not a technique as such but more an attitude or 'way of being' that we can develop over time and with practice.

Mindfulness is about bringing ourselves into the here-and-now and through curiosity and inquiry to start noticing what is happening inside and around us. The practice encourages a gradual shift from being in automatic pilot mode to conscious awareness, neither trying to hold onto what we like or to push away what we don't like. By teaching us to immerse ourselves in the present, mindfulness acts as a counter to both worry (which is future oriented) and rumination (dwelling on the past). Mindfulness involves acceptance, meaning that we pay attention to our thoughts and feelings without judging them – without believing there is a right or wrong way to think or feel in a given moment.

COMPASSIONATE WISDOM

His Holiness the Dalai Llama reminds us that in the Buddhist tradition both wisdom (which is connected with mindfulness) and compassion (which is connected with kindness) are needed to ease our own

suffering and for us to help others. He likens these qualities to two wings of a bird, or two wheels of a cart, saying that the bird cannot fly and the cart cannot roll with just the one.

Wisdom is about opening our eyes and seeing things as they are, recognising the interdependent and constantly changing nature of people, things and events. It is about seeing that genuine happiness does not depend on external circumstances but comes from deep within us. Wisdom may be achieved through the practice of mindfulness, which asks us to focus on what is happening in the present moment. Compassion involves a wish for freedom from suffering, both for ourselves and for others, recognising that we all want to be happy and avoid misery. Kindness is fundamental to compassion, along with qualities such as warmth, acceptance and love – they are all inextricably linked. In fact His Holiness the Dalai Lama is famous for saying that his 'religion' is kindness, and that there is no need for temples or any complicated philosophy: '*Your own mind, your own heart is the temple. Your philosophy is simple kindness*.'

Meditating and the brain

MRI (brain scan) studies suggest that regular mindfulness meditation reliably and profoundly alters the structure and function of the brain to improve the quality of both thought and feeling. Research also shows that compassion-focused mindfulness increases the capacity for empathy and social connectedness as well as positive emotions, such as love, joy, gratitude and contentment.

'Mindfulness itself is an act of kindness, of compassion. It teaches us about directing the capacity for compassion that we all have in ourselves.'

FLORIAN RUTHS

LOVING-KINDNESS

While mindfulness is important for alerting us to what is happening (becoming mindful), it is compassion or loving-kindness that holds the key to healing and transformation: without it lasting change is not possible. The word 'compassion' is derived from the Latin roots *pati* (to suffer) and *com* (with). In his book *Overcoming Depression* clinical psychologist Paul Gilbert defines it as, '*...basic kindness, with deep awareness of the suffering of oneself and other living beings, coupled with the wish and effort to alleviate it.*' There is an active component to basic kindness or compassion that involves the intention to reach out to others in order to reduce suffering. As Desmond Tutu notes this means there is an altruistic component to compassion that is not just feeling 'with' someone but is seeking to improve the situation. We can also take a compassionate stance towards ourselves.

> '*Ask yourself: Have you been kind today? Make kindness your daily modus operandi and change your world.*'
>
> ANNIE LENNOX

WHAT IS AND IS NOT MINDFULNESS

Mindfulness is not about living in an idealised floaty world where we all spend hours in a zoned-out state; nor is it about being endlessly and annoyingly positive, or hugging trees or losing our capacity to think. It is not something anyone 'does' to us, and does not involve signing up to a religion or buying into a set of beliefs. It is also not about relaxation (although this may be a side effect). Mindfulness is an experiential method for training the mind: it does use formal and informal mindfulness meditation practices; it does encourage self-acceptance; it does focus on developing self-awareness, and cultivating the ability to deliberately pay attention to whatever is happening (positive or negative) in the present moment. And adding compassion or kindness into the mix means treating ourselves and others with patience, gentleness and respect.

THE POWER OF THE MIND

Mindfulness recognises that the focus of our attention stimulates different brain systems and emotions: for example studies show that when we start thinking about certain foods, the body starts to produce a physical and emotional response connected to our experience of that food. You can try this yourself with the 'lemon' exercise on the following page.

TRY THIS: IMAGINING A LEMON

Imagine you are holding a slice of lemon. What does it feel like between your fingers or in your hand? Is it warm, cool, smooth, sticky? Now imagine bringing the lemon up to your nose. What does it smell like? Imagine touching the lemon with the tip of your tongue. What was that like?

Finally imagine putting the piece of lemon in your mouth. How do you experience that? Do you notice any bodily sensations or movements (maybe there is an increase in saliva for example or you find yourself screwing up your face at the imagined sourness). Can you describe the thoughts, feelings and sensations you noticed at each part of the exercise?

This simple exercise with an everyday object demonstrates the power of the mind. Simply by thinking about something we are able to 'conjure' a range of thoughts, feelings and bodily sensations. This means we can use the power of the mind and our imagination to our advantage by purposefully directing our attention onto thoughts and intentions of kindness and compassion. This is at the root of loving-kindness practice.

THE CHALLENGES OF MINDFULNESS

It is relatively easy to maintain a steady 'non-attached' awareness of our thoughts and feelings when these are relatively benign. But when we are going through a difficult time or when painful memories from the past come to the forefront of the mind it is much more difficult to simply 'be with' the images, thoughts and feelings that arise. The same is true in fact when feelings of intense pleasure or joy are stimulated, such as when we fall in love, or get the college grades or home or job we want. When we experience extremes of emotion the tendency is to 'over-identify' (the polar opposite of mindfulness) and we lose ourselves in emotional reactivity, trying to either hold on to the good feelings or push away the bad ones.

This is especially problematic when we experience powerful emotions such as grief and shame, particularly when these are accompanied by self-criticism and self-loathing, when it becomes almost impossible to maintain a dispassionate 'mindful' awareness. And unfortunately most of us are all too familiar with self-criticism, the negative messages that

'Mindfulness is simply being aware of what is happening right now without wishing it were different. Enjoying the pleasant without holding on when it changes.'

JAMES BARAZ

we use to put ourselves down. We call ourselves 'stupid' or 'silly', tell ourselves we are too this or that (too fat/too thin/too ugly/too much/too young/too old … the list is endless), that we don't deserve to be happy, that no one will like us, or we berate ourselves when we make a mistake and so it goes on.

This type of negative self-talk stimulates the threat system and puts us under stress. Instead what is called for is gentleness, kindness and self-compassion, in order to stimulate the self-soothing system and bring ourselves back into balance.

MINDFULNESS IN SOCIETY

In its present secularised form, the practice of mindfulness owes much to the pioneering work of John Kabat-Zinn and his work at the Stress Reduction Clinic at the University of Massachusetts. The success of the Mindfulness-Based Stress Reduction (MBSR) programme, started by Kabat-Zinn in 1979, initiated further research in the fields of clinical psychology and psychiatry. Studies show that other benefits of mindfulness include boosting the immune system and encouraging left-brain activity, the side most associated with wellbeing.

In Britain today the National Health Service uses mindfulness as a 'treatment' to help alleviate symptoms of anxiety and for relapse prevention in depression. As well as healthcare, mindfulness programmes are also used in the criminal justice system, in education, by the military and in business. Increasingly there is a growing recognition of the link between mindfulness and compassion and its associated qualities of kindness, warmth, and empathy, generating further research and new approaches within the helping professions. Compassion has become a focus of research with bodies such as the Compassionate Mind Foundation, set up to promote wellbeing through the understanding and application of compassion.

Compassionate-based mindfulness programmes can help people suffering with trauma and severe mental health difficulties, particularly those that are accompanied by high levels of shame and self-criticism. A key component of this is compassionate mind training, promoting healing and a sense of connectedness.

A LOVING-KINDNESS MEDITATION

There are many different types of mindfulness practice but essentially they can be thought of as formal, semi-formal or informal. Choose the approach that best suits your lifestyle and time available.

Formal practice involves setting time aside to sit (or lie) for an extended period (20-plus minutes), semi-formal also involves purposefully setting time aside but is shorter than a full practice, while informal practices are those that you can do on the move, bringing mindfulness into your daily routine, while you are walking, eating, exercising or in the middle of a complex task for example. The recommendation is little and often, so while long practices are obviously good, they need to fit in with your lifestyle.

This simple mediation is a cornerstone of Buddhist practice, designed to cultivate 'metta', which means loving-kindness or friendship. It is a concentration exercise which means we continually bring our attention back to the chosen object of focus (in this case spoken phrases) when the mind wanders off. The practice has been shown to have great healing and restorative power when practised regularly. Allow 20 minutes for the meditation.

1 Sit or lie comfortably where you won't be disturbed. Notice where your body makes contact with the chair or floor and feel the sensations in your body. Close your eyes and observe your breathing for a few rounds of the breath, allowing it to settle.

2 Reminding yourself that every living being wants to be happy and at peace, place your hands on your heart and silently repeat the following four phrases, holding them in mindful awareness and connecting to each of them in turn. Let each phrase mean what it says. You can repeat it to reinforce it, *May I be safe, May I be happy, May I be healthy, May I be at ease...*

3 When your mind wanders (as it surely will), gently bring it back and focus on the phrases. Don't be frustrated, it is normal for minds to wander. Instead congratulate yourself for noticing, and coax your attention back to the practice. If you find it difficult to connect with the meaning of the words or everything becomes vague and woolly, focus attention on your breathing and reconnect with the phrases.

4 Each time we repeat these phrases, we are harnessing the power of intention, which is the most important thing about the practice. You can make up your own phrases, but keep to the same structure. For example:

May I live in safety,
May I live in peace and joy,
May I enjoy physical health and wellbeing,
May I live with ease.

5 If you notice tension or tightness at any point then it is an indication that you are trying too hard. Take a deep breath and let it all go on the outbreath. Let the practice be easy. Imagine that sitting with yourself is like sitting with a close friend.

6 To bring the practice to a close, gently open your eyes and have a stretch, congratulating yourself for taking the time to take care of yourself in this way.

Remember: there are no expectations about how we are supposed to feel. Sharon Salzburg, a Buddhist practitioner and teacher on loving-kindness has said that it works even if we don't feel a thing! The main thing is to keep doing it.

'It is about learning how to be kind not only to ourselves but also to others, so promoting healing and a sense of connectedness rather than isolation ...'

BRANCHES
PATHWAYS TO KINDNESS

'If you want to do your best
for future generations of humanity,
for your friends and family,
you must begin by taking good care
of yourself'.

TARTHANG TULKU RINPOCHE

DEVELOPING *self-compassion*

SELF-COMPASSION

When things get tough in our lives we are often hard on ourselves, most of us finding it easier to be kinder to others than to ourselves, as if we don't deserve support or feel we are to blame for the things that are happening.

In bad times, according to psychologist and mindfulness teacher, Christopher Germer, we tend to become self-critical and isolated, and he argues that these reactions make things much worse for us and harder to find a solution. For unless we actively do something to change it, most of us are battling with ourselves, caught in a 'trance of unworthiness', a vice-like grip of negativity arising from a deep-seated inner belief that there is something fundamentally wrong with us, a phenomenon that many professionals believe has reached epidemic proportions.

Research indicates however that self-compassion promotes psychological resilience, wellbeing and a sense of connectedness. Self-compassionate

people seem more able to deal with life's setbacks and misfortunes, and to see mistakes as opportunities for learning. Their self-esteem is less related to external factors and evaluations by others but is more rooted within themselves, to feeling good from the inside.

Furthermore, the more genuinely openhearted and kindly disposed we are to ourselves, the greater is our capacity to connect with others with warmth and

Acting from the heart

Self-compassion is about moving our focus down from the head and into the heart. It is about allowing feelings of tenderness, sympathy, forgiveness and love which first we must give to ourselves before we can truly give them to others.

loving-kindness. As we develop a greater tolerance and acceptance of our own difficulties it is much easier to see others for who they really are; we are no longer projecting the unowned parts of ourselves onto them. It can also be a humbling and equalizing experience, as coming to terms with our own imperfections makes it easier to accept imperfections in others.

HOW SELF-COMPASSIONATE ARE YOU?

Dr Kristin Neff, a psychologist at the University of Texas in Austin, has developed a research tool called the Self-Compassion Scale that is being widely used in studies on self-compassion. For fun try taking the test to get a sense of your current level of self-compassion at www.self-compassion.org. Repeat it periodically to see if you notice any changes after you have been putting some of the ideas in this book into practice.

Neff identifies three main components to self-compassion: mindfulness, common humanity and self-kindness. The self-compassion scale measures these areas together with their polar opposites: mindfulness vs over-identification; common humanity vs isolation; and self-kindness vs self-judgement.

Try this: Three-minute compassion break
When you are feeling stressed or are in a difficult situation try this short three-minute exercise. It is inspired by Kristin Neff's three components of self-compassion.

1 Mindfulness: Notice where you feel the discomfort in your body and the thoughts and feelings you are having. Think or say to yourself: '*This is a moment of suffering*'.

2 Shared humanity: Remind yourself that you are not alone in feeling like this, many people have felt this way. Think or say to yourself: '*Suffering is part of life.*'

3 Self-kindness: Remember that being harsh and critical with yourself is not going to help. Instead you need to be kind to yourself. Think or say to yourself: '*I am doing my best, I am OK just the way I am.*'

THE TRANCE OF UNWORTHINESS

If we believe that at rock bottom we are not worthy of love or kindness we live our lives stuck in constricting beliefs, emotions and body sensations. Mindfulness practitioner and Buddhist teacher Tara Brach refers to this as the 'trance of unworthiness', which she claims we are all in the grip of to a greater or lesser extent. Signs of this include having a critical inner voice, feelings of fear and shame, experiencing knots of panic and anxiety in our gut, or feeling the heavy weight of depression in our bodies. We fend off this sense of unworthiness in different ways: for example, spending all our time trying to prove ourselves; disengaging from life because we are too scared we will fail; or addiction (whether through drink, drugs,

Try this: RAIN practice

This is a short informal mindfulness practice that is designed to stop us being so hard on ourselves. It was developed by Tara Brach who believes that we need to actively take care of ourselves before kindness and compassion can flourish. RAIN practice has four steps:

R: Recognise what is going on.
A: Allow the experience to just be there, whatever it is.
I: Investigate with kindness.
N: Natural loving awareness: this is the 'treasure' or fruit of the practice, which arises when we follow the first three steps.

Qualities of compassion

Kindness: This infuses everything to do with compassion.

Warmth: This is the emotional 'tone' we bring to everything.

Non-judgemental acceptance: This increases tolerance of difficulties and brings understanding whereas judgement is shame-inducing and causes us to shut down.

Strength: Having compassion means being strong enough to face our difficulties fairly and squarely instead of burying our heads in the sand.

Courage: Involves owning up and taking responsibility for what we have said and done, particularly when it has not been something nice.

Wisdom: It is not always easy to know what is the right thing to do or say, but wisdom is a quality that we can develop over time, through recognising when we have done something wrong and letting ourselves learn from our mistakes.

shopping, or gambling, for example), seeking the high that makes us feel better and masks the pain momentarily until it wears off and we have to do it all over again.

Through developing self-compassion and practising mindfulness we are able to gradually release ourselves from these false beliefs and unhelpful behaviours, reorienting ourselves towards learning to listen to ourselves and trusting our inner voice. The RAIN practice is a way of softening and opening the heart.

BLOCKS AND BARRIERS

When we start trying to become more kind and compassionate with ourselves we will run up against the negative beliefs and self-judgements that we hold about ourselves: that we are unworthy, that we don't deserve it, that it's selfish. Kindness can also stimulate the threat system.

We can hit a wall of fear – that if we start becoming more soft we won't be able to get on in the world. We fear that if we become 'too kind' then other people will take advantage of us, that we won't be able to say no. Feelings of kindness and warmth can also trigger memories of early attachment problems when maybe we didn't feel safe or our needs weren't met.

These beliefs and fears arise through having internalised the beliefs and expectations of others and the values of the culture we live in, as well as our early experiences. There is no need to fight against this: simply recognising, allowing, and investigating with kindness will start loosening the grip of these judgements.

THE WAY OF KINDNESS PRACTICE

It's not only during difficult periods of our life that we need to become more self-compassionate. When you notice you are being tough or hard on yourself at any time, take some time out and follow the 'way of kindness'.

When you find yourself being over-critical, deciding that your reaction to something is 'wrong' or berating and judging yourself for any reason, try and follow these steps to foster a more kindly approach.

1 Take kind advice: Take a deep breath, pause and think about what your best friend would say to you. Or what you would say if this was happening to your best friend.

2 Cultivate balanced thinking: Remind yourself that being self-critical and judging is not going to help. In fact it's only going to make you feel worse. Remind yourself that your thoughts and feelings have the power to make you feel good or bad. Try to see the whole picture in the situation and create a balanced view.

3 Be in the moment: Take each day, each hour, each moment, as it comes. What's happened can't be changed. What happens next can be determined by what happens now. Let go of past and future and relax into the now.

4 Attention switch: When you are focusing on the negatives, remind yourself of your positive qualities and the positive things that are in your life.

5 Comfort and soothe yourself: It is best to know beforehand what things you find comforting. A simple technique is to put your hands on your heart and say to yourself, *'It's ok …(your name), you are doing your best.'*

6 Make a collection of things you find comforting and soothing: It might be a piece of music, or looking at familiar or beautiful photographs. Remind yourself what it is you find soothing.

Learning how to 'befriend' ourselves is a way of developing a more compassionate relationship to ourselves.

Try this: Creating a kindness box

Rather like a memory box, a kindness box is a physical container that holds reminders of all the things that you find comforting and calming. You could make it from an old shoebox that you cover in nice paper or you could buy a box or tin

that you like. Into the box you can put things that make you feel happy and have positive memories associated with them – an old soft toy, a poem, photographs, postcards, theatre tickets, dried rose petals or a lavender bag for example. You could also create a list of phrases that you can repeat as you look through the box. Here are some suggestions, you can add your own:

• Pain and suffering is part of life.

• Bad things happen to everyone.

• This is a difficult moment, it will pass.

• I will get through it.

• May I be kind to myself.

• May I give myself compassion.

SOOTHING RHYTHM BREATHING

When we are tense, anxious or in pain, our breathing tends to become restricted and we 'over breathe'. Being able to breathe fully and deeply in a calm and soothing rhythm stimulates the parasympathetic nervous system and the area of the brain connected with compassion and kindness.

1 Close your eyes and bring your awareness to your breath; notice the coolness of the air as it enters your nostrils. Breathing out, notice the warmth of the air as it leaves your nostrils.

2 Continue breathing in and out in a relaxed way, noticing the sensations of the breath as it enters and leaves the body in

a soothing rhythm, like gentle waves washing onto and away from the shore. When you feel ready, open your eyes.

You can also practise mindfulness of breath informally by bringing your awareness to the breath for a few moments while you are going about your daily activities. It is a good idea to do this anyway; it will create a pause and help you to pace yourself better.

MY COMPASSIONATE SELF

Have you ever wondered what a more compassionate version of yourself would look like? In what ways would you and your life be different to how things are now? Compassion-focused trauma expert, Deborah Lee and colleagues suggest breaking your life down into different domains and to keep asking yourself the question, 'How can I build on compassion for myself and others?'

As a starting point, imagine how you would like things to be, as that is the first step to building a higher level of compassion. For example when thinking about work, ask yourself what sort of work you enjoy or is valuable to you. Are you doing what you like? What would make it better? Or when thinking about family and parenting, think about how you would like to be as a parent, and what will support you to achieve your goal.

Try this: Be your own best friend

Self-acceptance and being kind to ourselves is often easier said than done. Learning how to befriend ourselves is a way of developing a more compassionate relationship with ourselves. The next time you are feeling unhappy and are struggling with self-criticism, self-punishment and self-rejection, try this:

1 Imagine what you would say if it was your best friend who was feeling like this. Ask yourself what you would say to them if they were with you, and write the words down.

2 As you develop the imaginary dialogue think about how you would speak to them: would it be in a warm and friendly tone of voice or would it be cool and abrasive? Would you take the time to listen or are you impatient to move on? Write it down.

3 Do you notice any difference in how you speak to your best friend and talk to yourself? Make a note of this.

4 What do you think might change if you treated yourself in the way you treat your best friend? Try it and see what happens.

BE KIND TO *your body*

LIFE'S GATEWAY

Until something goes wrong with our physical bodies and we become ill or are in pain, we tend to take our bodies for granted and perhaps fail to give them the loving care and attention they need.

The body is our gateway to life and, regardless of whether or not we consciously remember them, it bears witness to every single one of our life's experiences. Developing kindness and compassion towards ourselves will help us become more aware and more in tune with our bodies, which can have a ripple effect on other aspects of physical care, include basics such as ensuring a healthy diet, taking regular exercise, having enough sleep, and keeping ourselves clean, warm and comfortable. We can also pamper our bodies with regular treats like taking a massage, enjoying a warm aromatherapy bath, going to the sauna or steam room, having enjoyable sex or relaxing in the warm sunshine. Bringing mindful attention to the body will help us develop a more kind and caring relationship with our bodies.

EATING MINDFULLY

In the developed world, obesity is on the rise. There are increasing concerns over the amount of sugar we are consuming, as well as processed foods, salt and saturated fat. Although at one level we all know that being overweight is not good for us – it puts strain on the heart and all the body's systems, making us feel tired, lethargic and depressing our mood – many of us find it difficult to gain control over what we eat and drink. We eat for 'comfort' and 'convenience', quickly grabbing the first thing we can find or that satisfies a craving. We use caffeinated drinks to perk us up through the day and alcohol to help us relax and unwind at the end of it. Every day we are making decisions that are not based on our nutritional needs but on eating habits influenced by our families and our culture.

Next time you cook a meal, pay attention at every stage of the process. Engage all your senses. When you are ready to eat the food, put it slowly into your mouth, and notice the sensations on your lips, tongue and teeth. Be mindful of your intention, savour each mouthful and notice when you feel full. At that point stop eating, as your body is telling you it has had enough.

> *Developing kindness and compassion towards ourselves will help us become more aware and more in tune with our bodies …*

EXERCISE KINDLY

No matter how busy and stressed out you are, it is worth making the time for regular exercise. Exercise helps to clear the mind: the less physical movement we take the more racing and busy the mind, whereas if we exercise we have a clearer head and are able to get things done more easily.

Exercise has many health-giving benefits. It releases endorphins, the body's natural painkillers, and has shown to be effective in alleviating symptoms of mild to moderate depression and anxiety. It also reduces blood pressure, encourages better sleep and improves physique. It is important to choose a type of exercise that you enjoy and can commit to making a regular part of your routine. You might consider walking, cycling, swimming, dancing, gardening, housework, low-impact aerobics, yoga and sports such as tennis or golf.

MINDFULNESS AND THE BODY

Bringing more awareness to the body is the foundation of mindfulness practice. It is perhaps easier to become aware of what is happening in the body, which is relatively slow and stable, than the mind – where thoughts come and go so quickly that it can be difficult to pay attention. Mindful attention can help make it easier to follow healthy eating or exercise plans. So while there is no direct evidence that meditation practice can help you lose weight, mindfulness helps us become more aware of our thoughts and actions, including those that relate to diet and exercise.

TIGHTENING VERSUS SOFTENING

Unfortunately when we have experiences we don't like, or we are under a lot of stress, we tend to unconsciously restrict our breathing and tighten up our muscles, creating physical tension and areas of tightness, which over time puts unnecessary stress on all the body systems and can develop into chronic pain and illness. A mindful response involves bringing awareness to the body, inviting ourselves to 'soften' and release, and using the breath to help us.

Body-kindness tips
- Drink plenty of water and include leafy green vegetables in your daily diet.
- Cut down on alcohol and caffeine.
- Take gentle exercise like yoga or Tai Chi to develop strength and flexibility.
- Stand tall or sit upright; good posture makes you look and feel confident.
- Take regular breaks away from your desk and stand or walk around.
- Remember to breathe properly.
- Smile even when you don't feel like it. Smiling or laughing releases 'feel good' chemicals and can improve your mood.
- Bring mindful attention to routine things; taking a shower, brushing your teeth, drying your hair. Notice the sensations.
- Have a set bedtime routine and use your bed for sleep and rest only. Do not eat, watch TV, go on your laptop or other mobile devices while in bed.

SOFTEN-AND-RELEASE ROUTINE

Sit or lie in a comfortable posture and bring your awareness to your breathing.

1 On the in-breath think or say to yourself 'soften', and as you breathe out think or say to yourself 'release'. Keep practising this until you gradually find your energy shifting from your head into your body.

2 Once you feel you are 'in' your body you can become more fully aware of the contact or pressure where you make connection with the chair and/or ground. Start to become aware of the sensations within the body beginning with the feet and working your way up through the body. Or let yourself be drawn to whichever part of the body is calling for your attention, and focus on that area, directing your breath to it, saying 'soothe' on the in-breath, and 'relax' on the out-breath. You are not trying to analyse or change anything, merely relaxing into whatever is there.

3 Now, bring your awareness to your body as a whole, visualising it sitting or lying in the room. Holding mindful attention of your whole body, expand your awareness to include the space surrounding your body, then beyond the room, softening and releasing into the space, expanding the awareness.

4 Now let go of the practice and any sense of trying to focus. Simply be where you are, allowing the body to breathe, letting thoughts and feelings come and go, like clouds passing through the sky.

THE COMPASSIONATE BODY SCAN

The body scan is a fundamental mindfulness practice. It involves mentally scanning or moving through the body, part by part, paying attention to each area in turn and noticing the sensations that come and go.

As well as developing mindfulness the body scan helps you deal with painful feelings instead of repressing them. This is important for developing compassion towards ourselves, being able to contain difficult feelings rather than avoiding them.

Find a comfortable place to lie down where you won't be disturbed; have a blanket or shawl handy if you get cold.

1 Close your eyes and focus on the rise and fall of the breath as it enters and leaves the body. Feel a sense of release and letting-go as you breathe out. Be aware of where your body makes contact with the floor or bed. Place your hands on your heart and take three deep breaths, stating the intention to be kind to yourself.

2 Rest your arms by your sides and imagine that your attention is infused with a soft, warm glow of compassion. There might be a colour that comes to mind. Bring the glow to the toes of each foot, note the sensations that you find there, then broaden your awareness to include the soles, heels, and top of the foot, the instep and ankle. Breathe into your feet on

the in-breath, and feel a softening and relaxing on the out-breath. Thank your feet for all that they do for you.

3 Gradually move the warm glow away from your feet up to your ankles, shins and calves, kneecaps and front and back of the thighs, breathing into each body part and softening and relaxing on the out breath. Give thanks for your legs.

4 Next move the glow of awareness up the body to the buttocks and pelvic region. If you are holding any tension here, use the breath to soften and relax. Hold the whole of your lower body in awareness and give thanks for everything it does.

5 Continue moving up the body, directing the soft glow of kind awareness to the abdomen, lower and upper back, shoulders, rib-cage and chest, pausing as you do so to bring a sense of tenderness and gratitude to each part you focus on.

6 When your mind drifts off (as it surely will) congratulate yourself for noticing and gently bring it back to the body. This will happen, but it does not mean you are getting it wrong, so don't berate yourself, just keep bringing the attention back.

7 Next take your gentle attention to the spine, feeling the points where it makes contact with the floor as well as the point where it meets the skull. Then bring your awareness down your arms and into your hands, the back of the hands, your palms, the fingers and the fingertips. Notice what the hands feel like, do both hands feel the same or is one side different to the other? Use your in-breath to soften and the out-breath to relax, taking the time to thank your hands for all the tasks that they do for you on a daily basis.

8 Slowly bring the warm glow of kindness to your neck, the back of the neck, the front of the neck, to your throat and face. Notice any areas of tension held in the face, in the jaw, around the mouth, around the eyes and forehead. Allow your face to relax and soften, see it infused with a warm glow and smile, holding your face in your awareness with loving kindness.

9 Take your attention up to the crown of your head then travel quickly back down to the soles of your feet. Imagine the breath entering your body through the soles of your feet and travelling up through the body and out through the crown of your head as though your body were a hollow bamboo through which the breath moves like the wind passing through trees. You can do this a few times, creating an awareness of the whole of your body breathing gently in a continuous cycle. Gradually feel a sense of peace calm, and gratitude infusing your whole body.

10 When you are ready to finish the practice, slowly bring your hands to your heart again and feel the warm glow, and appreciate yourself for taking the time to complete this practice.

11 Slowly start moving your body from side to side, take a yawn and a stretch, and turn over onto your right side before gradually sitting up. Sit still for a moment, taking your time and being gentle with yourself before standing and coming back into normal awareness.

COMPASSIONATE *mind*

COMPASSIONATE THINKING

The way we think influences the way we feel and how we react to different situations. Having kind thoughts and developing a compassionate mind is fundamental to fostering greater kindness.

A compassionate mind is an expansive, open state where we can flourish. This is relatively easy to achieve when we feel safe, happy and at peace. In such a state our hearts can open and the healing energy of loving-kindness can gently flow in and out of us as naturally and effortlessly as breathing. But when a tsunami of worry and negative self-talk disturbs our peace of mind it is more difficult. We become anxious and/or depressed, stressed and unhappy and may start doing things in an effort to escape our own minds. But with conscious intent we can change self-criticism into kindness and compassion for ourselves. With practise and commitment, this helps to rewire our thinking patterns along more positive and constructive lines and builds emotional resilience.

In his book *Hardwiring Happiness* neuropsychologist Rick Hanson says the human brain has a 'negativity bias', likening it to Velcro for negative experiences and Teflon for positive ones. This is because the human brain is programmed first and foremost for survival, the 'threat system' having

evolved to alert us to danger so that we can take appropriate action (fight, flight, freeze or appease). In modern urban society many of the everyday 'dangers' that activate the threat system are not actually life-threatening but are based on distorted perception, negative thoughts and unhelpful beliefs. Consequently developing a compassionate-mind means working against our natural biases and engaging the 'higher' brain's capacity to reason and think things through and to feel kindness and empathy for ourselves rather than beating ourselves up.

AUTOMATIC THINKING
Most of our thoughts are generated automatically, based on a mindset that has developed over time, creating well-trod pathways in the brain's neural circuitry. Automatic thoughts are our habitual responses and predispose us to see things a certain way. This may be either positive or negative, a sort of 'glass half full' or 'glass half empty' type of thinking. Through recognising negative automatic thoughts (NATs), psychologists have identified several typical thinking habits or patterns. Try and identify a negative reaction, step back and put it into perspective, then replace it with positivity. By stepping back you will stop yourself getting stuck in a temporary reaction, be able to put it into perspective, and then replace the negativity with an awareness that in time you won't feel so strongly about it, and something else will happen to make you feel happy and fulfilled.

TRY THIS: CHANGING YOUR MIND

In cognitive behavioural therapy (CBT) one of the ways to work with NATs is to keep a thought diary in which you notice and name the thought, and then change your mind by generating new, more helpful thoughts that offer a more balanced perspective. In doing this you are taking control of your mind and rewiring your brain by forming helpful thinking habits. This will create new neural pathways that will help to develop a more compassionate mindset that supports you rather than making you feel bad.

When there is a negative situation in your life, such as being overlooked for promotion for example, examine what it is you are saying to yourself when you are focusing on being upset/angry. If you are struggling with the feeling that the situation is unfair, and it's part of a pattern in which you never 'get what you want' or that you 'deserve better', step back and put things into a larger perspective. Ask yourself what is the worst that can happen in this situation? How do you think you will view it in six months' time? When you have thought that through, add in a new, kinder, more balanced thought, for example, 'It's natural to feel upset for a while, in time I won't feel so strongly. It doesn't mean I will never get what I want.'

THOUGHT DIARY

Thinking habit	Example of thought	Compassionate mind alternative
Black and white ('all or nothing') thinking	If I don't get that job I have failed.	There is a lot of competition for jobs. I did well to get an interview.
Thinking the worst ('catastrophising')	I keep getting headaches, I must have a brain tumour.	Perhaps my body is dehydrated and I need to drink more water.
Ignoring the positives and focusing on the negatives ('Eeyore' thinking)	So what that I've unpacked my boxes, there's still stacks to do.	I have made a good start and am doing things a step at a time.
Taking it personally	My friend ignored me when she walked past me in the street.	Maybe she had other things on her mind or didn't see me.
Predicting the future	It didn't work out in my last relationship so it won't this time.	Just because it happened last time does not mean it will happen again. I have changed a lot since then.
Mind reading	I know they don't like me.	I don't know this. I am not a mind reader.
Shoulds, oughts, musts	I must always be on time.	I can only do my best.
If I think/feel it, it must be true	I think something bad is bound to happen.	I am feeling anxious but that does not mean what I am thinking is true.

QUIETENING THE MIND

There are various ways we can learn to quieten the mind and instill a sense of calm. The best time to do this is before we start spiralling out of control so that we have some resources to draw on.

We all have bottom line or core beliefs, which act like a filter or lens through which we interpret information. These mental patterns get hardwired into the brain in the first months and years of life, making them very entrenched, with a tendency to be absolute. Our core beliefs give rise to the rules, demands and assumptions we live by (for example, 'I must always be on time') which in turn produce automatic thoughts that just pop into our minds when confronted with a situation.

Core beliefs are not always negative: good experiences of life and other people lead to healthy ideas about ourselves, others and the world. But the beliefs that cause emotional problems and activate the brain's 'threat system' – rather than the calm zone of kindness and compassion – are negative, for example, beliefs such as 'I'm unlovable,' or 'I expect people to treat me unfairly,' or 'life is difficult.' They also tend to become more evident when we are going through a difficult time, which is when we start to criticise and punish ourselves.

Calming the mind

One of the most compassionate and kind ways of dealing with upsetting thoughts is not to deny having them, or to fight against them but to simply acknowledge that they are there, to say to yourself, '*Right now I am thinking (say whatever it is you are thinking); just because I am thinking this does not mean it is true or will happen, a thought is just a thought, it is a mental event, thoughts come and go.*'

WORRY AND RUMINATION

Sometimes however we cannot switch off our thoughts and stop ourselves from worrying or ruminating. Worrying is future oriented (thinking about what might happen) while rumination involves the past (going over and over what has already happened). A way of working with worries is to take a logical, step by step approach, breaking the problem down into something specific and then following a pathway of choices. You can also try the following visualisation.

VISUALISATION: FALLING WORRY LEAVES

Get into a comfortable sitting position and close your eyes. In your mind's eye visualise a large, sturdy tree. This tree is ancient. It has stood for hundreds of years and has witnessed the coming and going of the seasons of the year. It provides shelter from the hot sun and has weathered many storms, driving rain, gale force winds, ice and snow.

• Deepening your breath, feel where your feet make contact with the ground and imagine that there are roots stretching down from the soles of your feet, reaching down into the earth.

• With each in-breath imagine that you and the tree are one, that at your core you are strong and steady just like a tree.

• As you continue to breathe, notice that the leaves on the tree are changing colour from green to red and beginning to fall.

• With each out-breath imagine that with each falling leaf you are letting go of worries and negative thoughts.

• As the 'worry leaves' drop you notice they land in a clear freshwater stream. Continuing to focus on the out-breath notice how the leaves float downstream on the current, moving further and further into the distance until the water runs clear.

• Stay with this sense of yourself as the tree and imagining the clear freshwater stream right by you. Notice how you feel in your body and mind.

• When you are ready, slowly open your eyes. Stretch and thank yourself for giving the time to this exercise.

THE WALL OF WISDOM

Another way to quieten the mind is to build a wall of wisdom that you can refer to when you are caught in a negative cycle of worry and self-criticism. The wall can take various forms, it can even just be inside your head.

Your wall should be made up of simple, repetitive phrases that you can use whenever one is needed. You can create the wall in a variety of ways, for example, stick post-it notes on a board in your bedroom, or even on the fridge, or else you could use a chalk board or white board and write the phrases on that, perhaps choosing a 'thought for the day' that you can repeat as a mantra at intervals throughout the day. Here are some examples of wise and soothing phrases to get you started.

• I say yes to myself.
• This too shall pass.
• I'm taking it a step at a time.
• I accept myself and all my thoughts.
• Thoughts are just thoughts, I am safe.
• I'm not the first human being that's felt this way and I probably won't be the last.
• Other people also struggle with self-criticism and negativity.

When you need to, say the phrase out loud, but make sure you speak in a warm, gentle tone. This helps to activate the vagus nerve and the parasympathetic nervous system, bringing kindness towards yourself.

BRINGING MINDFUL ATTENTION

Through regular mindfulness practice we are training ourselves to bring attention and awareness into the present moment, so that gradually worrying and rumination will start to slow down or stop altogether. But we need to allow this to be a sort of by-product or side effect of our

---

Try this: the STOP Technique

This is a classic informal mindfulness practice that you can use anytime to interrupt a stress cycle and to bring yourself into the moment. It can be done in a few minutes or less.

S = Stop. Stop whatever you are doing right now.

T = Take a few deep breaths.

O = Observe. What am I experiencing in my body, in my emotions, in my thoughts? What is going on in my mind? Is it busy or is it calm?

P = Pause: what is the most important thing for me to pay attention to right now? And when it feels ok … Proceed.

mindfulness practice rather than making it a goal or aim, for as soon as we do that then we are no longer dropping into what we are experiencing, but are struggling to make ourselves try and get somewhere.

Mindfulness practice does not have to be formal. You can use simple short techniques such as mindful awareness of breath, soothing rhythm breathing, or the STOP technique in the midst of activity, all of which give you a bit of space to reflect.

Through regular mindfulness practice we are training ourselves to bring attention and awareness into the present moment …

TRY THIS: CLOUD VISUALISATION

The breath helps to anchor the mind, giving it a 'neutral' focus that is calm and steady. By focusing on its rhythm we can calm our mind and cultivate detachment.

1 Sit in a comfortable posture, close your eyes and focus on the breath coming in and going out.

2 As you breathe bring awareness to your thoughts. See them as clouds passing through the 'sky' of the mind. As you watch your thoughts notice how the 'sky' changes: perhaps it is heavy with dark stormy clouds, or perhaps fluffy white clouds are moving slowly across.

3 Notice the changes in your body sensations and emotions as the 'clouds' move, using your breath as a focus. When you are ready, open your eyes.

BEFRIENDING *feelings*

BEING WITH DIFFICULT FEELINGS

When we are unable to tolerate difficult emotions we create difficulties in our relationships and with ourselves. Forgiveness and acceptance allow us to deal with troubled feelings in a healing and transformative way.

Pain and suffering is part of the human predicament and to a greater or lesser extent we all struggle with these feelings. Those with a lot of emotional intensity, such as anger, jealousy, fear or shame for instance, are associated with the threat system. Furthermore as we start to become more self-aware it can seem as though things are getting worse. It is a bit like going into a dark basement and gradually turning up the light so that we start to see more and more of what is in there, including all the junk. Instead of switching off the light and rushing back out the door, the most kind and caring thing we can do for ourselves ultimately is

to keep the light on and practise staying in the room, a bit like the adage, 'Face the fear and do it anyway.' We do this bit-by-bit, gradually building tolerance and emotional resilience and increasing our capacity to cope with difficult feelings.

It is easy to get caught in negative spirals of anger, hatred, resentment and a desire for revenge, then feeling guilty because we feel that way. We can become overwhelmed by our grief and sorrow or get stuck in fear and anxiety, unable to feel the feelings or let them go. These are all common, understandable and perfectly normal emotional states, part and parcel of being a human being, often serving a

> *'Pain helps. When we're open to pain, compassion flows like water down a mountainside.'*
>
> CHRISTOPHER GERMER

useful function: for example, fear is a signal of danger, or sadness a disconnection in our relationships. Yet it can be difficult to allow ourselves to experience the intensity of emotions and to be with our pain without judgement or feeling the need to do something about it.

The typical response to a feeling that we don't like and judge as 'bad' is to try and protect ourselves from it. We do this in a variety of ways, through what psychologists refer to as 'defence mechanisms'. For example we might try to repress or deny our sadness, push the feelings away, ignore them and soldier on, or else we might displace our feelings on to someone or something else through the psychological mechanism known as 'projection'. How many times for example have you found yourself getting into an argument with your partner only to realise later that the problem had nothing to do with them but was because you were feeling angry or upset about something

else? The opposite of projection is 'introjection', where we turn our feelings inwards and against ourselves, leading to self-loathing, self-rejection and even an annihilation of the self, so that we feel and behave as though we barely exist and do not matter at all.

Forgiveness and acceptance however are two connected qualities that allow us to deal with difficult feelings in a way that is healing and transformative. For when we can truly forgive others and ourselves in a way that is genuine (and not simulated) and openheartedly accept ourselves, warts and all, then we have the potential for something different or better. As psychologist Carl Rogers (1959) notes, *'The curious paradox of life is that when I accept myself just as I am, then I can change.'*

NON-JUDGEMENTAL ACCEPTANCE

Being able to avoid condemning ourselves (or others), and to let go of any angry desire to attack and be critical, is important if we are going to start becoming more self-accepting. The more we criticise and berate ourselves for feeling the way we do, the worse we feel. Like forgiveness however, genuine self-acceptance is not something that happens instantly or can be faked, but is something we might need to work at and return to over and over again.

THE COMPASSIONATE FRIEND

If we find it hard to be kind and non-judgemental towards ourselves we can visualise a compassionate friend to help us, someone who is kind and wise and accepts us the way we are. This can be based on a real person you know, or someone you construct in your mind.

1 Think about a problem that makes you feel bad about yourself – this could be something to do with your job, family or relationships, or perhaps a self-image problem that is affecting you negatively.

Meditation, familiarisation and cultivation

In Tibetan Buddhism the term 'meditation' also means both 'familiarisation' and 'cultivation'. Similarly a compassion-based mindful approach teaches us how to care for ourselves emotionally by becoming familiar with and learning how to 'befriend' our difficult feelings and to be aware of the pain, while also cultivating positive states of mind.

2 Make a note of what emotions come up when you think about this and see where you experience them in your body.

3 Now imagine that you have a compassionate friend, someone you can always turn to for support when things get difficult. This might be an actual person or it might be 'a higher power' such as God, or higher self or a guardian angel or even a literary character; it does not matter. You can create the figure in any way that feels right for you. This person knows your life history and understands your current circumstances, they know all your strengths and weaknesses and accept you the way you are, knowing that we all have our limitations.

4 Start a conversation in your mind with your compassionate friend by telling them how you are feeling. Imagine them replying. What do they say? How do they convey their kindness and concern for you? What words do they use? What does their voice sound like? Do they give you any advice on what do do or what strategies you might use to improve the way you feel about yourself? How does this help?

Try this: the SAFE Technique

Feelings of safety are associated with the 'contentment and soothing' system and can help bring distressing feelings into a more manageable zone. When feelings seem threatening and overwhelming, try the SAFE technique. It will help to bring you into the 'here and now' and to remind you of your connection with others. Take a quiet moment to go through the four stages of thoughts and feelings.

S = Soften into this moment: use the outbreath to soften and release.

A = Allow yourself to be with your experience just as it is, without needing to change it.

F = Feelings: pay attention to your feelings, and investigate what it is that you need.

E = Extend: remind yourself that everyone has problems, and extend thoughts of loving kindness to yourself and others.

'GIVING AND TAKING' MEDITATION
This Tonglen meditation focuses on accepting difficult feelings and generating wellbeing. In the Tibetan language, *tong* means 'giving' and *len* means 'taking'. Tonglen is a meditation practice that switches the usual practice of releasing negativity on the out-breath, encouraging us instead to breathe in the difficulties, challenging our tendencies to resist.

1 Sit or lie quietly in a comfortable position and close your eyes. Take a few breaths and imagine yourself breathing through the pores of your body until your attention is anchored in your breathing.

2 Next bring your awareness to your heart area and notice any sense of discomfort or emotional distress. Before labelling it, see if you can be with it. Ask yourself what does it feel like in your body? Does it have a colour? Or a texture? How big is it? When you have a sense of it as a 'thing' or entity you can give it a name (anger, sadness, fear, or hopelessness, for example).

3 Next link the discomfort to your breath, and on each in-breath imagine that you are pulling in the distress towards your heart, seeing it as a colour or a physical sensation or the name of the feeling. You can place your hands on your heart and say, 'Welcome' as you breathe it in.

4 In the space between the in-breath and out-breath imagine the discomfort being transformed by the loving kindness of your welcome and open heart.

5 On the out-breath, breathe out feelings of well being and relief from suffering. Let it be the opposite of the in-breath, so if you were breathing in darkness, breathe out light, or if you were breathing in anger breathe out kindness, or if it was anxiety breathe out calm. Just do the opposite of whatever you were breathing in.

6 Practise breathing in suffering and exhaling wellbeing until you get used to it, and keep this rhythm going, breathing in distress and breathing out kindness and wellbeing to yourself and others. When you are done, gradually open your eyes and sit quietly, allowing your inner experience to be exactly the way it is.

'Compassionate emotions are linked to feelings of warmth, support, validation, encouragement and kindness.'

DR DEBORAH LEE

NURTURING THE POSITIVE

As well as negative emotions we also have a great capacity for positive feelings such as love and affection, kindness and empathy, or joy and wonder. These are the feelings associated with the contentment and soothing system that make us feel happy and at peace with ourselves, connected to others and the environment. Happy people are more resilient when disaster strikes, enjoy more satisfactory relationships, and are more likely to succeed at work. Research also shows that emotions are essentially habits that we can either strengthen or weaken according to where we put our energy and attention. Positive emotions arise naturally when we can be in the moment and say 'yes' to whatever is happening without resistance, even when it is a negative feeling such as anger or jealousy or guilt. For it is not the feeling itself that creates the problem but the associated mental activity such as ruminating and worrying, combined with a resistance to experiencing the feeling and then letting it go that is problematic.

Being defensive against our pain means the barriers we put up also keep the good stuff out. The next time someone pays you a compliment, for example, notice whether you let it in or whether instead you shrug it off, change the subject or make a joke. We may also avoid happiness and good feelings because we fear loss. For example, some

people won't allow themselves to get into a close and intimate relationship through fear of abandonment or rejection, choosing to either stay alone or to select

---

I can wade Grief –
Whole Pools of it –
I'm used to that –
But the least push of Joy
Breaks up my feet –
And I tip-drunken –

EMILY DICKINSON

---

a partner where the feelings are more lukewarm – a sort of damage limitation approach should the relationship end or go wrong. As Emily Dickinson's poem says, we get used to our negative feelings and in some sense they become easier than becoming happy and joyful.

> **Try this: the Power of B.R.E.A.T.H**
>
> According to neuroscientist Alan Watkins, smooth, rhythmic breathing that is focused on the heart not only generates feelings of calm and contentment but also optimises performance so that we can 'be brilliant every day'. The length of the breath is less important than the rhythm, which needs to be paced and smooth. Focusing attention on the heart connects it to the brain, increasing positive feelings and self-confidence. By focusing on positive outcomes as we breathe, we also direct our intention towards our heart's desire.
>
> **B**: Breathe
> **R**: Regularly
> **E**: Evenly
> **A**: And
> **T**: Through the
> **H**: Heart every day

HAPPINESS INTERVENTIONS

Here are a few things to add into your week, that can bring happiness into your life. Helping others is a great way to also help ourselves to feel better.

• Make a decision that every day you will do at least one thing to help someone else – this could be something as simple as giving up your seat on the train, carrying someone's shopping bags, or volunteering to help in a community event.

• Make a list of your strengths and positive qualities. Pick one of these and try practising it in a new and different way every day for a week and notice the effect it has on your mood.

• Practise gratitude. Every day list five things that you are grateful for.

• The next time someone is nice to you – pause, take a breath and notice how it feels in your body, notice what thoughts pass through your mind, and how you feel. Practise doing this until you can stay relaxed and open when people are nice to you, and you can let in the good.

• Devote some time each day to self-care. Spend 15-20 minutes every day doing something to be kind to yourself.

• Do loving-kindness meditation every day.

FOOD FOR *the soul*

SPIRITUAL EVOLUTION

Many people believe that the human race is at a critical point, faced with a choice between evolving into higher levels of consciousness, or continuing along a well-trodden path towards self-destruction.

Qualities such as kindness, compassion, peace and love are seen as virtues in many cultures and religions. These qualities have an ethical dimension that encourages us to live from the heart rather than the head, and to extend beyond our petty concerns and ourselves towards others and a bigger picture. Yet for many people the idea of religion or spirituality has negative connotations and we struggle to define precisely what it is we believe or don't believe in. Whether or not we choose to follow a particular religion or spiritual path however, having some sort of inner or spiritual life can help us feel more connected with ourselves, with others and with the environment in ways that are pro-social and improve wellbeing. It is up to us to decide how we are going to do this.

The feeling that we are at crisis point as a species is what provided the impetus for the New Age movement where, dissatisfied with what mainstream culture and religion had to offer, many people turned to the East and 'discovered' ancient practices such as yoga and meditation. There has also been a

> *'Love what you do. If you haven't found it yet, keep looking. Don't settle. As with all matters of the heart, you'll know when you find it.'*
>
> STEVE JOBS

resurgence of interest in the old pre-Christian religions like Paganism or the Shamanic practices of indigenous peoples which honour the cycles of nature and our connection with the Earth.

For others, it has been a time for renewal of faith and a deeper commitment to an existing religious practice or else a conversion to a new faith, with stories in the news for example of Christians converting to Islam and vice versa.

It also accounts for the recent explosion of interest in mindfulness, with the suggestion that people have been 'starving' for an approach to spirituality that does not depend on catechism or belief, but is based on personal inquiry and experience. We can also understand this from the perspective of evolutionary biology. The prefrontal cortex or 'higher' brain is the most recently evolved part of the human brain and is active in states of gratitude, compassion, kindness and spiritual contemplation or meditation.

Developing a meaningful spiritual practice demonstrates our commitment to developing a society that is based on pro-social collective values, where people are more self-aware, more kind and compassionate, more trusting and forgiving, and where there is more love, peace and happiness in the world. To do this involves us taking personal responsibility for moving things forward rather than believing that there is a 'higher power' that will intervene and do it for us.

NOURISHING THE SOUL

Spiritual self-care is about deciding on the values that are important to us and then giving these attention and time so that they grow in us. Our values influence how we spend our time and time is a limited and precious resource – minutes become hours become days become weeks, then months and years – and before we know it we realise whole decades of our life have disappeared in a meaningless haze. If we don't make a conscious choice about where our values lie and what it is we love to do, whether we like it or not, we are soaking up the dominant ways of thinking embedded in mainstream consumer society – 'me' first, pleasure seeking, materialism, the drive for power and status – and living a life according to other people's values rather than our own.

IDENTIFYING VALUES
Knowing what our values are can help shape our life in the ways that are most important to us.

1 To identify your values ask yourself this question: 'What is truly important to me in my life right now?' Be as honest as you can and without thinking too much about it, make a list.

Examples of values:

Security	Trust
Being myself	Love
Intimacy	Peace
Self care	Helping others
Adventure	Eating nice food
Being healthy	Material comforts
Success	Wealth
Fun	Career or work
Self-awareness	Living in the present
Meditation practice	Friendships
Being outside	Being the best

2 The next step is to sort your list and prioritise each item.

3 Now look at your list again and ask yourself how much time you actually give to what you value and how much you are distracted with things that don't really align with your values. Can you make any changes to help redress the balance, even in small ways?

SWEETGRASS – HERB OF KINDNESS
Also known as holy grass, manna grass, Mary's grass, peace grass and unity grass, sweetgrass (*Hierochloe odorata* or *Anthoxanthum nitens*) is an aromatic herb native to northern Eurasia and North America. In some shamanic traditions, sweetgrass is one of four sacred medicine plants (the others being cedar, tobacco

Spiritual life
Studies have shown that having religious beliefs can prolong the life of people who are suffering. You don't have to be religious to see life as a gift but there is research that suggests people who do see life as a gift tend to be healthier than their non-religious counterparts.

and sage) often used in ceremonies for calming, healing and purification.

Among indigenous peoples sweetgrass is said to represent the sacred hair of Mother Earth and is linked to love and kindness for all people everywhere. Sweetgrass is often braided into three strands to represent love, kindness and honesty, and the coming together of many hearts into one. When sweetgrass is used in a healing or talking circle, it is said to have a calming effect and is used to attract positive energy or Spirit. In northern Europe sweetgrass was strewn before church doors on Saints' days, its aroma being released when trodden on.

SMUDGING

The practice of smudging is used in many cultures and religions to cleanse and purify and to open up the psychic space for connection with a higher power. This could mean God, the divine, the whole, Spirit, all that is, everyone everywhere – use whatever concept works for you. You could even think of it as helping to strengthen the connection with your kind and compassionate self.

The practice involves burning incense or sacred herbs and using the smoke to clear negativity around the body's aura or magnetic energy field and to bring vision. It is also used to purify sacred instruments and to clear sacred space before

ceremonies. In ancient Greece, smudging formed part of the rituals to contact the dead after periods of fasting and silence.

If you like rituals and find them helpful, you can try your own smudging ceremony. If you cannot get hold of a smudge stick or bundle you could use incense instead.

Light the smudge stick or incense and hold it in front of you. Using your hands or a feather, fan the smoke over you, starting above the top of your head and moving down your whole body.

When you have 'cleansed' yourself with the smoke affirm your intention for loving kindness with the following prayer:

May I and all living beings be safe
May I and all living beings be happy
May I and living beings be healthy and live
 in love
May I and all living beings be at peace.

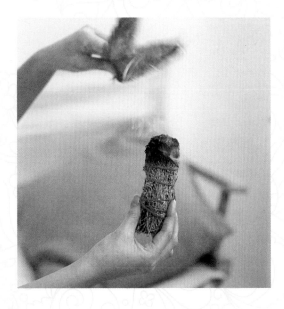

Mantras

A mantra is a repetitive phrase or sound that is spoken during meditation or prayer to align our thoughts and intentions with our 'higher' self, or the Divine. In Tibet, many Buddhists carve mantras into rock as a form of meditation. Here are some of the most frequently used.

Om: this is one of the earliest known mantras, dating back some 3000 years to the Vedic tradition in India. The meaning of Om is difficult to translate but it can be thought of as 'the source of all that is'.

Om Mani Padme Hum: a Buddhist mantra that again is difficult to translate but is said by the Dalai Lama to have the potential to transform body, speech and mind.

Om Namaha Shivaya: this is one of the most important Hindu mantras. Like Om Mani Padme Hum, it is also said to have transformative power. It roughly translates as 'I bow to the Absolute Reality' but it can mean 'Praise be to God'.

Sh'ma Yisrael, Adonai Eloheinu, Adonai Echad: a well-known prayer that is central to Jewish faith: 'Listen Israel, Adonai is our God, Adonai is One'. The prayer is said silently and synchronised with the breath.

Not my will but Thy will be done: words taken from the Lord's Prayer in the Christian tradition, denoting that we align our will with God, letting God direct our lives.

Bismillah Al-Rahman, Al-Rahim: in Islam, a mantra meaning in the name of Allah, the most compassionate, the most merciful.

HEARTFULNESS AND THE SPIRIT

In many Asian languages the word for 'mind' and for 'heart' are the same. Mindfulness practitioners such as Jack Kornfield and Jon Kabat-Zinn for instance have said that heartfulness might be a more appropriate term than mindfulness. This slight change of emphasis goes beneath all the hype to remind us of the deeper, some might say spiritual dimension of mindfulness, which is maintaining a deep intimacy with the awareness of our own being, with the spirit or essence of who we really are, moment by moment. This level of mindfulness goes beyond ego or selfhood, the narrative of 'I', 'me' and 'mine', offering an experience of the self that is much more fluid, open and responsive than something fixed, solid and full of certainty.

HEARTFUL MINDFULNESS

The bottom line is that mindfulness and spirituality are not separate activities but offer a holistic perspective where everything is connected. For essentially mindfulness, or heartfulness, is about being in relationship – with ourselves, with others, to whatever unfolds, to the 'whole'. It means opening the heart and allowing 'whatever is' to be there, with qualities like loving-kindness and compassion gradually developing in us as a sort of by-product and rippling out to touch others who come into contact with us.

The real practice of mindfulness is about how we live our lives, moment to moment, and not just when we are on the mat, with life itself being the teacher.

It is possible to be mindful at work, at play, in our relationships, while cooking and eating, while walking, taking a shower, doing a workout, doing pretty much anything. Mindfulness allows us to be present for life as it is, to live the life we have. It is not asking us to go to the church, temple, monastery or a particular building or place. And it is not about achieving a special state we might call enlightenment or heaven or even well-being.

Mindfulness simply asks us to be, to take a pause and bring awareness to whatever is happening, to inhabit the present moment, breath by breath. It asks us to engage with the life we have, so that the focus becomes life before, rather than after, death.

GIVE THANKS FOR YOUR BLESSINGS
Whether we follow a recognised religious path or have a non-secular approach, seeing life as a gift and being thankful for all we have been given is a spiritual activity if it is heartfelt and genuine. Here are some ideas for creating an attitude of gratitude.

At the beginning and end of every day close your eyes, place your hands in namaste or prayer position and say to yourself, 'I give thanks for …'. Feel the meaning of what you are saying without trying to force anything.

Write a thank you letter to someone who has been important and helped you in your life. Think of all the important people in your life. Each day pick one person and make a list of how they have helped you. Write a thanksgiving poem or paint a picture that expresses your gratitude.

HEALING LIGHT MEDITATION

No matter what your spiritual belief, light is a universal symbol for qualities such as truth, wisdom, compassion and kindness. Light a candle and set it before you.

• Sit comfortably and take a few relaxing breaths. With a soft-focused gaze look at the candle and observe the warm glow of its flickering light. You may keep the soft gaze for the whole meditation or else close your eyes if that feels more comfortable.

• As you breathe in imagine you are drawing the flame into your heart and visualise a warm soft glow of light in and around your heart area. On the out-breath

visualise the light around your heart area expanding, radiating kindness.

• Continue to visualise the light entering your heart, expanding and softening and then allowing it to spread through the body until you feel as though you are bathed in light and infused with kindness.

• Now focusing on the out-breath imagine that your body is like a beacon, its healing light expanding and radiating out beyond you to include others in your home, your town, your country, and the entire world.

• Continue to visualise yourself and your surroundings bathed in radiant light. When you are ready, slowly open your eyes.

THANKSGIVING

Small ways I am grateful …
The smell of fresh coffee
The sweet taste of mangoes
The warmth of a
lover's touch
The howl of the wind
Clouds racing across the sky
The hush of snowflakes falling
The sound of silence.

RAJE AIREY

FRUIT AND SEEDS
SPREADING KINDNESS

The very nature of kindness is to spread.
If you are kind to others,
today they will be kind to you
and tomorrow to somebody else.

SRI CHIMNOY

KINDNESS AND
relationships

KIND RELATIONSHIPS

Kindness has the potential to improve our relationships, reducing emotional distance between people and helping us feel more connected. This includes relationships with those with whom we experience difficulty.

Back in 17th-century England, the poet John Donne wrote 'no man is an island', in recognition that human beings exist in relationship to one another. Quantum physics has advanced our knowledge about the interconnectedness of all life so that the idea that we are lone identities who function independently does not hold water. However, while relationships are a potential source of joy and fulfillment they also bring pain and frustration and can be a source of stress. In the famous words of Sartre, 'The other is hell', or as author Douglas Adams has said, 'People are a problem'.

> *'Not only is empathy hard to outsource and automate, but it makes the world a better place.'*
>
> DANIEL PINK

Relationships and health

Studies show that strong relationships are a better predictor of a healthy heart than factors like poor diet, smoking, obesity and lack of exercise. Isolation and lack of meaningful relationships can turn ordinary unhappiness into despair or dread and is one of the underlying factors in depression and other mental health problems.

THE POWER OF EMPATHY

Empathy creates a bridge between people, allowing us to see the world through another's eyes. Through empathy we are able to develop compassion and loving kindness, recognising the other as a person and not as a commodity.

When we lack empathy we find it difficult to respect differences and accept that other people's feelings and needs are as valid as ours. We can objectify people, making it easier to judge and mistreat them. Seeing ourselves as separate and disconnected we view others as potential competitors for jobs, housing, partners, or money, as obstructions that get in our way, or as adversaries who threaten our beliefs and ways of seeing the world.

RELATIONSHIP MAP

A relationship map is a powerful way of getting an insight into your relational world. This method uses found objects to create a 3D visual representation. Using objects rather than drawings means you have the flexibility to move people around.

You will need: an assortment of found objects (for example, pebbles, stones, shells, feathers); a clear worktop (such as a tabletop, large tray, the floor); phone, tablet or pen and paper.

1 Without thinking too much about it, choose one of your objects to represent yourself and place it on your worktop.

2 Next make a list of the people who 'populate' your life: this might include parents, partners, ex-partners, in-laws, children, friends, colleagues, neighbours.

3 Pick an object to represent the people on your list and place it on your worktop. If there are groups of people who fall into a category (for example work colleagues), you can pick one object to represent the group unless you want to represent a particular individual.

4 When you are satisfied everyone is represented, sit back and look at where you have placed the objects. Maybe some are quite close to you, others are further away; maybe some are in little groups or some are out on a limb. Is everyone in the right place? If not, make any adjustments.

5 Now think about the image you have just created. What thoughts and feelings were evoked as you did it? Why did you choose the objects that you did? What does each say about the person they represent? And how do you feel about the map now it's done? Make a note of your reflections and notice if there's anything that strikes you in particular or if there is anything you would like to be different.

6 Take a photograph or make a sketch of your work so you can refer to it later.

7 Repeat this exercise on a regular basis and notice if there are any changes in the positioning of the objects as well as in the type of objects you choose. Once again capture your feelings and thoughts about it so that you can refer back.

KIND COMMUNICATION

The way we communicate with others, even if not overtly threatening, is often a form of subtle aggression and manipulation. It can be rare to deeply or genuinely listen to one another from the heart.

How we relate to others has a huge impact on how we feel. We are unlikely to feel good if we spend our time undermining others, lying or cheating, or if we get what we want through bullying and coercion. Being on the receiving end of this kind of communication doesn't make us feel great either, inducing feelings of fear, guilt, shame, anger, resentment and so forth. However, we do have a choice: we can either go with 'threat' based motives or 'compassion' based motives, depending on what we want to cultivate.

NON-VIOLENT COMMUNICATION

In the 1960s, American psychologist Marshall Rosenberg developed a communication process known as non-violent communication (NVC), which has been used in education, parenting, and in conflict zones around the world, including Rwanda, Serbia and the Middle East. NVC is based on an assumption that people are compassionate and kind by nature, that we all share the same basic human needs and are 'wired' to get our needs met.

'When our communication supports compassionate giving and receiving, happiness replaces violence and grieving.'

MARSHALL B. ROSENBERG

Non-violent communication teaches that 'violent' communication (whether psychological or physical) is based on instilling fear, attempting to dominate and imposing retribution, with one party (or both) trying to control or take revenge on the other. Violent communication is a learned behaviour that is culturally embedded, picked up through social interaction, and will stimulate the threat system. NVC on the other hand is based on co-operation, compassion and mutual respect. It takes a partnership approach to problem solving and focuses on three areas, self-empathy, empathy and honest self-expression, and will stimulate the soothing system.

HOW TO PRACTISE NVC

To put the principles of non-violent communication into practice involves a commitment to developing your self-awareness and being really honest.

• Think of a relationship where you want to improve your communication.

• The next time you have an interaction ask yourself: What was my intention here? Was it to get them to do what I want or to make them see my point of view? Or was it to try to improve our relationship?

• When listening, ask yourself: Am I truly listening and genuinely interested in what they are saying? Or am I so busy formulating what I want to say that I haven't really been paying attention?

• How genuine and sincere am I? Does what I say 'match' with what is going on inside me or am I feeling/thinking one thing but saying or doing another?

• What is it like to feel deeply heard and understood? How far was I able to offer this in this interaction? Has there been any 'shift' in the relationship?

COMPASSIONATE PARENTING

As adults it is easy to forget how big and powerful we are in comparison to our children, not only physically but also psychologically. And easy too to forget that treating children like 'mini-adults', appealing to their reason before their higher brain is fully developed, is a waste of time. Instead we need to meet our children on their terms, put ourselves in their shoes and to speak gently and warmly from an open and loving heart.

One of the most nourishing ways of being with our children and giving them the type of attention they deserve is through play. But in our busy lives it's hard to find time to really play with them on their terms and to show how much we like being with them. You just have to count how many times you say 'no' compared to 'yes' in one day. Or how often you say 'in a minute' but that minute never comes.

Try setting aside special time each day when you let your child know that for the next 20 minutes this is their time. Follow their lead and let them be cleverer or more competent than you. Simply giving your child your undivided attention and showing your enthusiasm in being with him or her is tremendously beneficial for both of you.

THE PRACTICE OF METTA

It is fairly easy to be empathic and kind towards the people in our circle of trust. But what about strangers? Or people we find difficult? Loving-kindness – called *metta* in Buddhist practice – encourages us to extend it to all people everywhere.

• Start by thinking about someone you genuinely care about, hold them in your mind's eye and send them loving-kindness by repeating the *metta* phrases:

May you be safe

May you be happy

May you be healthy

May you be free from suffering

• Do this for a few different people, perhaps thinking of someone who is not well or is struggling in some way and needs extra support. Holding them in awareness, repeat the *metta* phrases.

• Now think about someone you don't know so well, someone who is neutral for whom you don't feel either a strong like or dislike. Usually we know few neutral people, as once we know someone we start to form an opinion. So you might have to think about strangers, the person you sat next to on the train or the homeless person you see on your way to work each day. The intention is to extend loving-kindness to people on the basis that they exist, and that everyone deserves it.

• Eventually and with practice you can begin to extend *metta* towards someone you dislike or with whom you have strong negative feelings. Do not pick the most difficult person straightaway but choose someone you find mildly difficult; this could be someone at work or in your social group for instance. With time and practice you may be able to include the most difficult people.

Remember that extending loving-kindness to someone we don't like does not mean that we condone their actions or think it doesn't matter that they hurt us or someone else. We do it because we realise that holding onto anger and resentment is actually hurting ourselves. By digging deep into our own hearts and extending loving-kindness to someone who has hurt us we are able to let go of our own suffering.

HEALING THE HEART

The ways we relate to the people around us have a physical effect on our well-being as well as an emotional one. Communicating honestly and letting go of negative emotions can actually improve our health.

FORGIVENESS

There is great healing power in the ability to genuinely forgive someone who has done you harm. Holding a grudge can increase blood pressure and puts strain on the heart whereas being able to forgive, if not necessarily forget, helps us move on, letting go of negative feelings and repairing ruptures in relationships. But for forgiveness to be therapeutic it needs to be genuine and not put on, to avoid resentment building up and leaking out in other ways.

'To be in the present with someone else is a gift. The gift of attention is perhaps the most precious and envied of all, even though we do not always realise it.'

PIERO FERRUCI

It is important too that no one should ever feel forced into thinking that they should or must forgive. And no one has the right to take the moral high ground over anyone else. Some wounds are so deep and the hurt and injustice so terrible that forgiveness is not always possible.

So first and foremost it is about accepting where we are without thinking we are 'wrong', and giving ourselves the time and space to feel the hurt and pain without trying to change anything. When we do this it's quite possible that genuine forgiveness will arise spontaneously without us needing to 'do' anything.

KINDNESS IN ACTION

• Say or do something nice for someone every day. Notice what is created between you and the other person as a result.

• Spend money on others – it doesn't need to be a lot, just the simple act of generosity makes us feel good as well as the other person.

• Practice loving-kindness meditation towards others as well as yourself.

• The next time you are in conversation with someone you find annoying or usually ignore, give them your full attention.

• The next time you are with someone when they are upset, don't try to fix it, make it better, or attempt to persuade them out of it, simply allow yourself to be with them, opening your heart with thoughts of loving kindness.

• Drop the need to be 'right' and practise listening from your heart instead.

• Be the person that makes others feel special. Be known for your kindness, understanding and empathy.

• Slow down … the more we hurry, the less we are willing to help.

KINDNESS
and society

KINDNESS INITIATIVES

Any act of kindness or compassion, big or small, makes a difference, whether it's one individual smiling at a stranger or an entire nation welcoming refugees fleeing from a crisis.

In a world where we have grown to be suspicious and mistrustful of others, where we make judgements based on people's religion, the colour of their skin, even the type of clothes they wear, or the extent to which we see them as 'one of us', we are faced with the challenge of how to create a more peaceful and tolerant society. This would be a world in which difference is celebrated rather than feared and where we are united by compassion and empathy for one another and ourselves. In the words of Martin Luther King: *'Darkness cannot drive out darkness; only light can do that. Hate cannot drive out hate; only love can do that.'*

Love and heart-felt qualities such as kindness, compassion, tolerance and

> *'Carry out a random act of kindness, with no expectation of reward, safe in the knowledge that someday someone might do the same for you.'*
>
> PRINCESS DIANA

respect for others, as well as the ability to deal with conflict in a non-violent, cooperative manner, comes from within the person. These qualities are not commodities to be bought or sold, nor are they beliefs that we can sign up to. Rather they are signs of the genuine moral development that grows through emotional intelligence, self-awareness and self-acceptance. Viewed in this context compassion-based mindfulness as well as

Kindess and familiarity

Findings suggest that the more people experience their similarities with one another the more likely they are to perform an act of kindness. Training in compassion-based mindfulness has been shown to increase people's willingness to help a stranger.

'random acts of kindness' become radical acts, having the potential to change society from the bottom up and from the inside out, one small step at a time.

Kindness is contagious. When we're kind we inspire others to be kind. Therefore we should pass it on, or 'pay it forward'. Like a stone dropping into a pond, kindness creates a ripple effect that spreads outwards to touch others, to a friend of a friend of a friend … known as the 'three degrees of separation' effect.

Based on the principle that kindness has healing power and is a potent force for change, the internationally recognised Random Acts of Kindness (RAK) Foundation is a not-for-profit organisation dedicated to providing tools and resources to promote acts of kindness. It gives daily RAK suggestions and promotes kindness initiatives such as '*Choose to be Nice*', reminding people that we all have a choice about how to 'be' in the world. The Foundation has also pioneered '*Creating Safe Spaces*', a bullying prevention toolkit for use in the classroom as well as the 21-day Kindness Challenge, where school children perform five acts of kindness every day for 21 school days.

> '*The best parts of a good life: little nameless unremembered acts of kindness and love.*'
>
> WILLIAM WORDSWORTH

Kindness cards

One way of spreading random acts of kindness (RAKs) is by using 'Kindness Cards'. The idea is that you think of an act of kindness, perform it (anonymously, ideally) and then leave the person a 'kindness card'. The person receiving the card is then expected to pass on the card by performing an act of kindness for someone else, and so on.

TRY THIS: PAY IT FORWARD
Here are some simple ideas to pay it forward. Pick one or make up your own and get started.
- Buy a coffee or cup of tea for someone you don't know.
- Leave flowers on your neighbour's doorstep.
- Mail a card to a friend.
- Take time to talk to the homeless person on the street.
- Share a positive blog post.
- Read to a child.
- Be polite, say thank you, smile a lot.
- Give a lift to someone who can't drive.
- Forgive mistakes.
- Listen from your heart.
- Make a random act of kindness list!

Caffè sospeso

The tradition of the *caffè sospeso* ('pending' or 'suspended' coffee) is said to have originated in the working class cafes of Naples in Italy. It is a simple idea. Customers ordering their coffee pay for extra drinks which can then be claimed for free by those in need. The donor and the recipient would remain unknown to one another to protect people's pride and dignity.

The *caffè sospeso* has come to represent a symbol of grassroots solidarity and was the inspiration for Suspended Coffees, a movement started by Mark Sweeney (a then unemployed father) in 2013. Soon Mark had over a quarter of a million followers on social media and thousands of cafes around the world had signed up to offer 'suspended coffee' in their businesses. Suspended Coffees is about more than just a cup of coffee however. It demonstrates the power of kindness to restore faith in humanity and has expanded its circle of influence to include social enterprise movements that provide coaching and mentoring to teens and young adults. It is also teaching entrepreneurial skills to empower people to get back on their feet, as well as inspiring people to perform 'random acts of kindness' and help people out.

I may not have appreciated the importance of kindness had I not experienced the lack of it. I grew up in a small town in Ireland, where I was faced with bullying, both physical and emotional violence and feelings of isolation. All my life I'd been told that I wasn't good enough and I'd never amount to anything. I had been a scared and lonely child, and those taunts had stayed with me into my adult life. … There is no act of kindness too small to help restore our faith in humanity, and that is what we're about … We can make all the difference in the world.

Mark Sweeney, Founder of Suspended Coffee (The Huffington Post, 2014)

**TRY THIS: THE THREE-MINUTE
BREATHING SPACE**

Use this mindfulness practice at intervals during your working day. It creates a pause if your thoughts are whizzing out of control and helps to bring you into the present. It encourages a compassionate and mindful stance and helps you deal better with the tasks in front of you. It has three steps, which you can think of in the shape of an hourglass figure.

1 Becoming aware: Either sitting or standing up straight, close your eyes (if possible) and bring awareness to your inner experience. Notice your thoughts, your feelings, and your body sensations.

2 Gathering and focusing attention:
Next narrow the focus of your attention to 'spotlight' on the breath. Notice the physical sensations of the breath as it enters the body, the rise and fall of the abdomen as you breathe in … and all the way out. Use the breath to anchor yourself in the present.

3 Expanding attention: Now expand your focus on the breathing to include a sense of the body as a whole, as if the whole body was breathing. Use the breath to soften into any areas of tension or discomfort, exploring and befriending the sensations. Finally expand your attention further to include the space around your body.

Work clever, work kind

This is about taking a step back, taking a pause and hitting the reset button. So during intense periods of work, even though you might think you don't have time, it is actually better to take breaks and allow your mind to clear. It is clever to be kind to yourself rather than 'pushing through' and working too hard.

KINDNESS IN LEADERSHIP

In many business organizations there is an assumption that negative feedback is the way to make employees more motivated and that if you are 'too' kind and forgiving you will be seen as weak. People also think that being too self-compassionate will make them lazy and that a certain level of fear and pressure is necessary for people to 'perform' in their jobs. However many forward-looking organizations are recognising the importance of creating a positive and supportive work environment through mindful leadership.

An example of this is the WakeUp Project in Australia. Founded by Jono Fisher, who wants to make Sydney the world's kindness capital, the WakeUp Project hosts events designed to inspire mindful leadership. Results show that creating a more mindful workforce helps to reduce stress, increases resilience, self-awareness, and compassion, and encourages people to innovate and inspire.

KINDNESS IN THE WORKPLACE

In today's tech-saturated world, many people feel overwhelmed, exhausted and disengaged and the workplace is often a place of stress. Aside from being in the 'wrong job', many difficulties relate to relationships with work colleagues, an unsatisfactory physical environment (lack of natural light, cramped conditions for example) and the organisational culture itself where workers may experience anything from lack of support and positive feedback to bullying and having unreasonable demands made on them. Introducing mindfulness as well as random acts of kindness into the workplace has been shown to generate positive feelings and be helpful in reducing stress.

Being happy at work makes good business sense with research showing that happy workers are three times more creative and productive than unhappy ones. The best workplaces are where people have shared goals and aims and work well together.

EMOTIONAL LITERACY

Traditionally our society has been afraid of emotion, and education has been more or less synonymous with the cultivation of the logical, mathematical, rational and linguistic 'intelligences'. Recognising that intelligence is actually multi-faceted, 'emotional intelligence' is now recognised as an important area, with the need to develop 'emotionally literate' citizens seen as important for a healthy society. Emotional literacy is now taught in many schools. It has three components: self-understanding; understanding and managing our emotions; and understanding social situations and managing relationships, which includes experiencing empathy for others and effective communication.

Some courses are now available that are designed to teach secular mindfulness to teachers, parents and students as a way to help develop emotionally literate, self-aware citizens. Results show reductions in stress, burnout and anxiety and better mental health.

TRY THIS: ACTS OF KINDNESS AT WORK

Think how much nicer the workplace would be if everyone was at least a little kinder. Try practising Random Acts of Kindness (RAK) at work and see what difference it makes. Here are some ideas:

• Bake some cookies for your colleagues.

• Leave a welcome message on the office whiteboard when you leave.

• Give someone a compliment or praise a colleague for something they have done.

• Leave coins and a pay it forward note in an envelope by a vending machine.

• Design and print Kindness Cards for employees to pass from one person to another to accompany each kind act.

• Create a RAK bulletin board for people to post their stories.

• Squash a rumour rather than gossip.

• Organise a shared lunch.

• Remember, everyone is doing their best.

• Perform loving kindness meditation on the colleagues who annoy you the most.

> *'The smallest act of kindness is worth more than the grandest intention.'*
>
> OSCAR WILDE

KINDNESS AND *the earth*

OUR RELATIONSHIP WITH NATURE

Kindness towards ourselves and to others needs to be extended to our surroundings and environment. We can't exist in a bubble, however successful we are in increasing kindness, if our planet is being destroyed.

Maybe there has never been a greater imperative for us to widen our circle of kindness and compassion than at this time. Habitat destruction, overharvesting and overhunting, unsustainable human population growth and pollution are all taking their toil on the natural environment. The list of plants and animals on the critically endangered species list for example has more than doubled in the last sixteen years. There is also evidence that the earth is warming. According to the US Environmental Protection Agency the average temperature rose by 1.5°F (-17°C) during the last century and is predicted to rise again in this one. Although these changes might sound trivial they translate to large and potentially dangerous shifts in climate and the weather: we have already begun to

Thich Nhat Hanh

Thich Nhat Hanh is a Zen Buddhist master, teacher, writer and peace activist who has been practising meditation and mindfulness for 70 years. Originally from Vietnam he established the Plum Village Community in France. Thay, as he is known to many thousands of his followers, believes that our addiction to consumerism arises from the lack of meaning and connection in our lives. He also believes a spiritual revolution is needed if we are to confront the multitude of environmental challenges facing us and civilisation is to survive.

'When we recognise the virtues, the talents, the beauty of Mother Earth, something is born in us, some kind of connection, love is born.'
Thich Nhat Hanh

witness the ice caps melting, rising sea levels, and extreme weather – floods, heat waves and droughts for instance.

For decades Thich Nhat Hanh (b.1926) has been a leading international figure campaigning for a radical shift in the way we think and act to address climate change and to change our relationship with nature. In 2014 he gave his *'Falling in Love with the Earth'* message to the United Nations and reminded us that many civilisations that have gone before us have been destroyed because they could not live in harmony with nature. Thich Nhat Hanh warns that if we continue with 'business as usual' we are on course to self-destruction and the human race will disappear from Earth. Forgoing our greed and selfish interest in continuing to gobble up the Earth's resources we need to become more mindful and create ripples of loving kindness that include the environment, the natural world and the Earth that is our home.

'There's a revolution that needs to happen and it starts from inside each one of us. We need to wake up and fall in love with the Earth. Our personal and collective happiness and survival depends on it.'

THICH NHAT HANH

'A human being is a part of the whole called by us the universe, a part limited in time and space. He experiences himself, his thoughts and feeling as something separated from the rest, a kind of optical delusion of his consciousness. This delusion is a kind of prison for us, restricting us to our personal desires and to affection for a few persons nearest to us. Our task must be to free ourselves from this prison by widening our circle of compassion to embrace all living creatures and the whole of nature in its beauty.'

ALBERT EINSTEIN

ONENESS WITH GAIA

Developed in the late 1960s by James Lovelock, a British scientist and inventor, Gaia theory proposes that the Earth and natural environment is a self-regulating, complex living system that supports life on the planet. The theory was named after Gaia (or Ge), the ancient Greek primeval deity of Earth who emerged at creation along with air, sea and sky.

Although many scientists disagree with key aspects of Gaia theory, the idea that the Earth is one giant self-organising system is now fairly mainstream. We recognise that the air, the ocean and the soil do not just provide an environment for life, but are a part of life itself. In this context Gaia is symbolic of a holistic view of life on Earth, where everything is interconnected and actions have a knock-on effect. This means that when any species becomes extinct we may also be destroying a part of ourselves, for we are also part of Gaia.

Recognising that people and the planet are connected, are one and the same rather than separate entities, may be important for changing our relationship with the Earth to one of loving kindness rather than greed and exploitation. This recognition is at the core of many indigenous traditions where sickness is connected with alienation from the Earth and where the healing of the people and the healing of the Earth are considered symbolic and go together.

Sangha

Breathing, sitting and walking mindfully all help to create an energy field or aura of mindfulness around us; the more people who deliberately practise this the bigger the energy field will become. It is also easier to make changes in our life if we are supported by other people rather than doing it in isolation on our own. So meet up with friends or look for like-minded people, and join or form community groups to support your compassion-based mindfulness practice and wish for greater harmony with the natural world. In Buddhism such a community is known as a 'sangha'.

NOURISHING THE SOUL

Nature has the capacity to inspire feelings of awe and wonder, feeding us at a soul-deep level. Being out in nature can also help us regain a sense of perspective on our lives by connecting to something bigger than us.

Maintaining our connection to the natural world is very important to well-being. Finding a beauty spot and purposefully taking an 'awe walk' not only helps us recharge our batteries but can also re-inspire our love and commitment for the Earth. Try writing down your thoughts and feelings before and after being in the countryside and notice what difference it makes to your mood.

THE WISDOM OF THE BEE

According to legend when bees die out, mankind will follow. Einstein gave humanity just four years to live if bees become extinct, while in the ancient world lands that flourished were linked to healthy bee populations.

Stretching back into the mists of time, the bee has been revered, imbued with symbolic meaning and associated with sacred tradition, prophecy and the occult (meaning 'hidden knowledge'), as well as with government, art and literature. In ancient Egypt for example, the bee was the symbol for Egypt and 'beekeeper' was the title given to Pharaoh. Bees also appear frequently in classical mythology where they are sometimes referred to as the 'birds of the muses', while evidence from Çatalhöyük, a Neolithic settlement and considered to be one of the world's oldest cities (dating back to nearly 7500BC), associates bees with fertility and the Great Goddess. Like ants, bees work in the spirit of co-operation rather than competition and they have an ancient reputation as the bringers of order. The bee hive is a symbol for a stable society founded on industry and collectivist values, and it is also a predominant symbol in Freemasonry.

Bees are remarkable. They pollinate plants and trees and produce honey, which has a range of amazing properties. Yet bee colonies are collapsing and bee populations all over the world are in decline.

To support bees and other wildlife we can create mini wildflower meadows in our gardens, allotments or backyards, or even in a window box. Wildflowers tend to prefer poor soil and a sunny site. Wildflowers or those that are native to a particular area and have not been cultivated or modified in any way, play an important role in biodiversity and balancing the ecosystem.

'The bee is more honoured than other animals, not because she labours, but because she labours for others. ... (she) works unceasingly for the good of the hive.'

ST JOHN CHRYSOSTOM (349–407 AD)

KINDNESS PLEDGES FOR THE EARTH

The culmination of loving-kindness practice is to focus on offering *metta* to all living things, all people everywhere, animals, plants and anything that is alive. You might even include the sun, moon and stars, the planets of our solar system and all the galaxies of the known universe and beyond.

Each one of us can commit to taking one small step to protect ourselves and life on Earth. The act maybe small but if it is done with the intention of spreading loving-kindness then like the 'butterfly effect' it can have the power to stimulate change on a bigger scale.

• Wear a green ribbon and show your solidarity with the Earth.
• Avoid food high in 'air miles'.
• Buy local, buy seasonal.
• Use your own fabric bags.
• Don't buy water in plastic bottles.
• Join a people's climate march.
• Turn off extra lights.
• Don't leave televisions or other kinds of electronic equipment on 'standby'.
• Eat less meat.
• Go vegetarian.
• Go vegan one day a week.
• Walk more and use the car less.
• Grow wildflowers.

TRY THIS: WALKING WITH KINDNESS

By practising loving-kindness meditation we connect with our love and compassion, and can become living, breathing manifestations of peace and kindness, right here, right now. If you have the opportunity, try this sequence outdoors, preferably in the countryside, to generate a greater sense of connection with the Earth. If you can, take off your shoes and walk barefoot. Whether you do the walk indoors or outside, barefoot or not, the basic sequence is the same.

1 Be aware of the contact of your feet with the ground or the earth, feeling its solidity beneath you. Co-ordinate your breathing with walking, breathing in for one step, breathing out for the next.

2 Each time you take a step, imagine you are gently peeling your foot off the ground, noticing the sensations as you lift it to take the next step.

3 Every now and again, widen the focus of attention to the environment and the world around you. Pause, notice the colours, shapes, textures. Breathe it all in with gratitude.

Breathing in, I know that I am breathing in.
Breathing out, I know that I am alive.
Breathing in, I know that I am peace.
Breathing out, I know that I am love.
Breathing in, I know the Earth and I are one.
Breathing out, I send loving-kindness to the Earth.

INDEX

This edition is published by Lorenz Books,
an imprint of Anness Publishing Ltd,
108 Great Russell Street,
London WC1B 3NA;
info@anness.com

www.lorenzbooks.com; www.annesspublishing.com; twitter: @Anness_Books

If you like the images in this book and would like to investigate using them for
publishing, promotions or advertising, please visit our website
www.practicalpictures.com for more information.

© Anness Publishing Ltd 2017

A CIP catalogue record for this book is available from the British Library.

Publisher: Joanna Lorenz
Senior Editor: Joanne Rippin
Designer: Nigel Partridge

PUBLISHER'S NOTE
The reader should not regard the recommendations, ideas and techniques expressed
and described in this book as substitutes for the advice of a qualified medical
practitioner or other qualified professional. Any use to which the recommendations,
ideas and techniques are put is at the reader's sole discretion and risk.

RAJE S. AIREY
Raje S. Airey is a UKCP registered psychotherapist and BACP accredited counsellor.
She works as Clinical Lead and offers therapy to people suffering with depression
and anxiety. She has also written and edited several books specialising in health and
lifestyle and has spent time in India studying meditation and Eastern philosophy.
She is currently developing her interest in compassion-based mindfulness
and its therapeutic applications.